Convergence Guidebook for Corporate Financial Reporting

Convergence Guidebook for Corporate Financial Reporting

BRUCE POUNDER

WILEY

John Wiley & Sons, Inc.

Published by John Wiley & Sons, Inc., Hoboken, New Jersey.
Published simultaneously in Canada.

For general information on our other products and services, or technical support, please
contact our Customer Care Department within the United States at (800) 762-2974,
outside the United States at (317) 572-3993 or fax (317) 572-4002.

Wiley also publishes its books in a variety of electronic formats. Some content that
appears in print may not be available in electronic books.

For more information about Wiley products, visit our web site at http://www.wiley.com.

Library of Congress Cataloging-in-Publication Data:

Pounder, Bruce.
   Convergence guidebook for corporate financial reporting / Bruce Pounder.
      p.   cm.
   Includes bibliographical references and index.
   ISBN 978-0-470-28587-9 (cloth)
   1. Accounting–Standards.   2. Corporations–Finance.   3. Financial statements.
I. Title.
   HF5626.P64 2009
   657′.3–dc22   2008048459

Printed in the United States of America.

10 9 8 7 6 5 4 3 2 1

To Roxane—
Words cannot describe how much I treasure what I have learned from you.

Contents

Acknowledgments

Writing this book has been a very personal journey. But I would not have had the opportunity to undertake the journey without the support that I received from Alfred M. King and Dennis Geyer. I am grateful to Al for opening so many doors for me, and I am indebted to Dennis for his timely words of encouragement.

I also wish to express my deep appreciation to Sheck Cho, my editor, for sharing my enthusiasm for this book—and for his patience as well.

To Al, Dennis, and Sheck—thanks.

Bruce Pounder

Preface

Everything you know about corporate financial reporting will become obsolete over the next ten years. The reason can be stated in one word: *Convergence*.

As commonly used by financial professionals, the word *Convergence* refers to the global convergence of financial reporting standards, a phenomenon that is causing increasingly profound changes in financial reporting in the United States and throughout the world. In the United States, Convergence is truly the "next big thing" in corporate financial reporting.

If you have managerial responsibility for the preparation of financial reports in accordance with U.S. generally accepted accounting principles (GAAP), then the *Convergence Guidebook for Corporate Financial Reporting* is for you. You will certainly benefit from this book if you hold a title such as chief financial officer, vice president of finance, controller, manager of financial reporting, or manager of accounting. Other professionals whose work is related to corporate financial reporting may also benefit from this book, for example, auditors, corporate compliance officers, investor relations officers, and accounting educators.

The *Convergence Guidebook* will help you prepare for the many new challenges that are resulting from Convergence. Specifically, this book will provide you with timely, practical guidance on preparing your department and company for the immediate and ongoing effects of Convergence. This book will also provide you with information that will help you remain employed and pursue new career opportunities as Convergence transforms labor markets in the United States and elsewhere.

This book is not a compilation of existing financial accounting or reporting standards. Nor is it a book on interpreting, applying, or implementing existing standards. And it is certainly not an academic textbook on financial reporting. In contrast, this book will:

- Explain the phenomenon of Convergence—what it is and what it is not.
- Explain how and why U.S. GAAP has changed and will continue to change as a result of Convergence.

- Explain how and why Convergence will alter U.S. labor markets for financial reporting talent.
- Explain the critical decisions and plans that managers must make in order to prepare their companies, their departments, and themselves for the growing impact of Convergence.
- Provide expert guidance on making and implementing critical decisions and plans in order to prevent Convergence from interfering with the attainment of company goals, department goals, and personal career goals.
- Describe the adverse consequences of delaying preparations for the impact of Convergence.

Bottom Line: The time to prepare for Convergence is now, and the information that you will need is in your hands.

PART I

Phenomenon of Convergence

In order to provide a solid foundation for the remainder of this book, Part One describes and explains the phenomenon of Convergence. This part consists of three chapters:

- Chapter 1 will introduce you to the phenomenon of Convergence.
- Chapter 2 will summarize how Convergence will impact U.S. companies and their financial managers.
- Chapter 3 will explain why you must prepare for Convergence now.

To get the maximum benefit from this book, be sure to read the preface, then read this part thoroughly. Your investment in understanding the origin, nature, and scope of Convergence, along with other fundamental concepts covered in this part, will be well rewarded as you continue through the rest of the book.

CHAPTER 1

Introduction to the Convergence of Financial Reporting Standards

This chapter provides an in-depth introduction to the phenomenon of Convergence. In this chapter, you will learn exactly what Convergence is—*and isn't*. You will also learn *why* Convergence is happening.

Financial Reporting Supply Chain

To understand the phenomenon of Convergence, it is helpful to begin by looking at the *financial reporting supply chain*, which refers to "the people and processes involved in the preparation, approval, audit, analysis and use of financial reports."[1] Just as the supply chain for tangible products is the network of parties that manufacture, inspect, distribute, and use the products, the financial reporting supply chain is the network of parties that prepare, audit, distribute, and use financial reports.

In the financial reporting supply chain, financial information flows through various stages. The flow of information starts with raw data about the financial effects of transactions and events on an enterprise. That raw data is processed progressively until it is eventually presented to end users in a highly filtered, summarized, and structured fashion.

As financial information flows from one stage to the next in the financial reporting supply chain, the various supply chain participants (preparers, auditors, etc.) add value to the information. This is analogous to the way in which manufacturers of tangible products add value to raw materials by transforming raw materials into finished goods, or the way in which distributors add value to finished goods by transporting specific goods to specific locations at specific times in order to meet the demand of end users.

While it is universally agreed that the financial reporting supply chain starts with the enterprises that prepare financial reports for use by parties outside of those enterprises, there is less agreement on who the primary end users of the financial reporting supply chain are. However, in the United States and increasingly throughout the world, the primary end users in the financial reporting supply chain are assumed to be investors and creditors, that is, individuals and institutions who seek to profit from allowing enterprises to use their financial capital.

In the United States, for example, the primary objective of external financial reporting is considered to be providing "information that is useful to present and potential investors and creditors and other users in making rational investment, credit, and similar decisions."[2] Of course, there are other users of financial reports, such as government agencies and academic researchers, who may use financial reports for different purposes. But meeting the information needs of such users is of secondary importance to meeting the information needs of investors and creditors.

Thus, the financial reporting supply chain exists in the United States and elsewhere in the world primarily to provide investors and creditors with information that is useful in making economic decisions about the allocation of capital to the enterprises that operate within our economy. Investors and creditors obviously benefit directly from the financial reporting supply chain, but it should be noted that a well-functioning financial reporting supply chain also serves the public interest. By helping investors and creditors to make sound capital allocation decisions, the financial reporting supply chain makes our economy more efficient at satisfying people's needs and wants with our scarce resources. This is true on a both a national and global scale.

Even though financial reports are only one source of information that investors and creditors use in making economic decisions, they are a very important source of information for the economic decisions that investors and creditors make. Many of the economic decisions made by investors and creditors result in transactions or events that are accounted for and reported by the enterprises in the financial reporting supply chain that prepare financial reports. But other economic decisions affect how the financial reporting supply chain itself works, that is, the ways in which supply chain participants add value to raw data about the transactions and events that enterprises account for and report.

One of the most pervasive ways in which economic decisions affect the working of the financial reporting supply chain is through the imposition of *standards* on the supply chain's participants (i.e., preparers, auditors, and distributors of financial reports), processes (i.e., preparing, auditing, and distributing financial reports), and products (i.e., information having specific content and format that is passed from one participant in the supply chain to the next). Today, the economic decisions that individuals and institutions are making with regard to financial reporting supply chain standards are causing those standards to change in the United States and throughout the world in profound ways. Because those economic decisions and the resulting changes in standards are the very essence of the process of Convergence, the next section of this chapter will further explore the role of standards in the financial reporting supply chain as well as the economic decisions that individuals and institutions make with regard to such standards.

Role of Standards in the Financial Reporting Supply Chain

Both users of financial reports and institutions that exist to serve the public interest have strong economic incentives to impose standards on the various participants, processes, and products of the financial reporting supply chain. For example:

- The existence and enforcement of high-quality financial reporting supply chain standards improves the usefulness of financial reports, and therefore helps investors and creditors make better economic decisions regarding the allocation of their capital. This in turn improves investors' and creditors' returns and makes our economy as a whole more efficient at satisfying people's needs and wants.
- The existence and enforcement of high-quality financial reporting supply chain standards lowers the risk that investors and creditors perceive to be associated with making capital allocation decisions, which provides investors and creditors with a greater number of less risky opportunities to deploy their capital profitably and which ultimately produces broad benefits to society from economic growth.

Thus, standards that pertain to the financial reporting supply chain have the potential to deliver significant economic benefits to both users of financial reports and society in general. But the economic benefits of standards do not come automatically. This is because standards do not occur naturally—they must be created and updated. Also, participants in the financial reporting supply chain cannot be relied on to comply automatically with pertinent standards—enforcement is needed. Without effective compliance enforcement, standards themselves have little value.

Because the activities of creating, updating, and enforcing standards require economic resources, those activities will not happen unless someone chooses to sacrifice economic resources in order to make them happen. Specifically, people who expect to benefit from the existence and enforcement of financial reporting supply chain standards must make economic decisions regarding how much of their scarce economic resources they are willing to sacrifice in order to obtain the benefits.

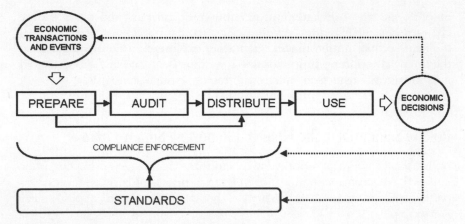

EXHIBIT 1.1 Financial Reporting Supply Chain

At this point, you may wish to review Exhibit 1.1 for a graphical summary of the financial reporting supply chain and the ways in which economic decision making by financial report users influences the supply chain through the existence and enforcement of standards.

Investors, creditors, and governmental bodies generally recognize that it is in their economic interest to sacrifice economic resources to some degree in order to develop, maintain, and enforce standards that apply to the financial reporting supply chain. In developed economies, standard-setting and standard-enforcing activities are typically carried out on behalf of investors, creditors, and the general public by formally organized bodies. Various funding mechanisms are employed to transfer economic resources from the beneficiaries of standards to standard-setting and standard-enforcing bodies.

In the United States, for example, the Financial Accounting Standards Board (FASB) is the recognized financial reporting standard setter for private-sector entities. Also, the U.S. Securities and Exchange Commission (SEC) enforces compliance with financial reporting standards by the entities that are under its jurisdiction (typically, those whose securities are issued to or exchanged among members of the general public).

Due to the existence of intermediaries such as the FASB and the SEC, most end users in the financial reporting supply chain do not participate directly in standard-setting and standard-enforcing activities. However, they generally have opportunities to participate indirectly through a "due process" that many intermediaries follow. Even though most end users in the financial reporting supply chain are not directly involved in the setting and enforcing of standards for the supply chain, it is important to recognize that standards are still set and enforced primarily to serve the information needs of those end users.

Of the many standards that pertain to the financial reporting supply chain, *financial reporting standards* are the most fundamental in terms of ensuring that the information needs of investors and creditors are met. Because financial reporting standards are at the center of the phenomenon of Convergence, the next section of this chapter will provide a working definition of the term *financial reporting standards* as that term will be used throughout the rest of the book.

Financial Reporting Standards

Financial reporting standards pertain specifically to *preparers* of financial reports, the *process of preparing* financial reports, and the *products of the preparation process* (e.g., traditional financial statements such as the balance sheet). Financial reporting standards are distinct from other standards such as auditing and distribution standards that pertain to participants, processes, and products downstream from the preparation stage in the financial reporting supply chain.

In common usage, the terms *financial accounting standards* and *financial reporting standards* are sometimes used interchangeably with each other and are sometimes used in contrast with each other. When used interchangeably with each other, both terms refer broadly to standards that pertain to any aspect of preparing financial reports. When used in contrast with each other, the term *financial accounting standards* refers specifically to standards for the recognition and measurement of items of economic significance, whereas the term *financial reporting standards* refers specifically to standards for the presentation and disclosure of recognized and measured items in financial reports.

Because there is little need to distinguish between "accounting" and "reporting" standards in this book, the term *financial reporting standards* as used throughout the book refers broadly to any prescriptive guidance that pertains to:

- Preparers of financial reports
- The process of accounting for items of financial significance
- The process of preparing financial reports
- The content of prepared financial reports
- The format of prepared financial reports

Understanding that financial reporting standards can and do differ throughout the world is essential to understanding the phenomenon of Convergence, and so the next section of this chapter will examine how financial reporting standards differ among countries.

How Financial Reporting Standards Differ among Countries

There are several dimensions on which financial reporting differs among countries. Naturally, the language (e.g., English, Spanish) and currency units (e.g., dollars, euros) used in financial reports vary from country to country. Standards that pertain to the financial reporting supply chain also differ among countries, as does the enforcement of compliance with those standards.

In particular, companies in different countries have traditionally used different country-specific sets of financial reporting standards in preparing financial reports. In some countries, companies are legally required to use a country-specific set of financial reporting standards. In other countries, companies have more freedom to choose the financial reporting standards that they use, but as a practical matter, companies within a country typically gravitate toward using the same set of standards—standards that often differ from the standards used in other countries.

Different sets of financial reporting standards often go by different names around the world. In the United States, financial reporting standards are collectively known as *generally accepted accounting principles* (GAAP). While many observers disagree with the characterization of U.S. standards as "principles," that is what our standards have traditionally been called.

Other countries, such as Canada, have also traditionally referred to their standards as *GAAP*. But, over time, many standard setters throughout the world have moved from referring to their standards as *GAAP* or *accounting principles* or even *accounting standards* in favor of the term *financial reporting standards*, which reflects the evolving sense that "accounting" and "reporting" standards are largely inseparable from each other in practice and that both kinds of standards exist to support sound, informative financial reporting as an end goal. As explained earlier, this book uses the term *financial reporting standards* in the same broadly inclusive way that the world's standard setters are increasingly using the term.

In addition to nominal differences in what financial reporting standards are called, there are many substantive ways in which financial reporting standards differ throughout the world:

- The expressed objectives of financial reporting (e.g., assumptions about end users and their information needs)
- The overall content of financial reports (e.g., which kinds of financial statements are required)
- Individual accounting and reporting provisions (e.g., recognition, measurement, presentation, disclosure)
- Influences on the standard-setting process (e.g., economic, cultural, governmental, business practices)

At this point in time, there are easily dozens of different sets of financial reporting standards in use throughout the world. However, two particular sets of standards have come to dominate the world's financial reporting landscape. The first is U.S. GAAP, a country-specific set of standards that is developed and maintained for U.S. private-sector reporting entities by the FASB. The other set is called *International Financial Reporting Standards*, officially abbreviated as *IFRSs*, although in the United States the name is almost always abbreviated as *IFRS*. Because this book is written primarily for a U.S. audience, the more common abbreviation *IFRS* is used in this book.

IFRS are developed and maintained by the International Accounting Standards Board (IASB). The IASB is the standard-setting arm of the International Accounting Standards Committee Foundation (*IASC Foundation* or *IASCF*), a not-for-profit entity incorporated in the United States. What makes IFRS unique is that unlike the many sets of country-specific financial reporting standards used throughout the world, IFRS are *country neutral*. In other words, IFRS are designed to be used by enterprises regardless of which country or countries the enterprises operate in. The fact that most of the world's countries use or have committed to use IFRS in the near future is an important aspect of the phenomenon of Convergence. But the growing use of IFRS throughout the world is not all there is to Convergence. In particular, Convergence in the United States is a much more complex phenomenon. So at this point, we turn to examine the phenomenon of Convergence from a U.S. perspective. Along the way, we will debunk several prevalent myths about Convergence, so be prepared to unlearn some things that you may think you know about Convergence.

What Convergence Is—and Is Not

With regard to financial reporting standards, the word *Convergence* has two related meanings. First, Convergence refers to the ongoing efforts of financial reporting standard setters in the United States and around the world to eliminate differences in financial reporting standards among countries. Second, Convergence refers to the absence of differences in financial reporting standards among countries. Thus, as reflected in those two meanings, Convergence is both a *process* and a *goal*.

The *process* of Convergence can and does occur in different ways, often simultaneously. *Set-level Convergence* occurs when companies in a country adopt an entire existing set of country-neutral standards that has been (or will be) adopted by companies in other countries. In contrast, *standard-level Convergence* occurs when standard setters change individual standards within each of their respective sets of standards in order to make the individual standards the same as each other.

There are two variants of standard-level Convergence. In the *unilateral* variant, a standard setter replaces one of its existing standards with a different existing standard from another set of standards. In the *multilateral* variant, each of several standard setters replaces an existing standard with a common one that is different from any of the standard setters' existing standards. In both variants, it is possible for financial reporting supply chain participants to perceive a replacement standard to be "better" or "worse" than the standard it replaced.

Standard-level Convergence is not the same as standard-level *harmonization*. Harmonization refers to a situation in which similar individual standards in two different sets of financial reporting standards are not identical to each other, but allow reporting entities to make accounting policy choices that satisfy both. In the past, global harmonization of financial reporting standards, rather than global Convergence, was viewed as a primary goal by the world's financial reporting standard setters. But over time, for various reasons, standard setters came to pursue the more beneficial goal of Convergence instead of harmonization.

Because the process of Convergence is focused on the development and universal adoption of country-neutral standards, and because a high-quality set of country-neutral standards—IFRS—already exists and its use is spreading to more and more countries, it is tempting to conclude that Convergence from a U.S. perspective is all about the point in time when companies in the United States will adopt existing IFRS. But that is not what Convergence is about from a U.S. perspective. The United States has experienced and will experience Convergence differently from other countries. As a result, we should not expect to simply replicate other countries' choices or experiences regarding Convergence.

For example, many countries outside of the United States have imposed mandatory set-level Convergence to current IFRS on listed companies. The most notable examples are the countries of the European Union (EU), which required listed companies to switch to IFRS starting in 2005. But in the United States, companies are extremely unlikely to experience mandatory set-level Convergence with current IFRS, for three main reasons:

1. Current IFRS are high-quality standards and are superior in quality to the country-specific financial reporting standards that they have replaced in many countries, but current IFRS are not demonstrably superior in quality to current U.S. GAAP.
2. Current IFRS as published by the IASB have been locally modified through political action in many jurisdictions, including the EU. The existence of country- or jurisdiction-specific exceptions is fundamentally incompatible with the goal of Convergence. Until such exceptions are eradicated, there is less incentive for the United States to "buy into" IFRS.

3. The IASB's current funding mechanism and governance are generally viewed as being in need of improvement before participants in the U.S. financial reporting supply chain would acknowledge the legitimacy of the IASB as an authoritative setter of financial reporting standards that would apply to U.S. companies.

Another way in which the United States is experiencing Convergence differently from other countries is the way in which standard-level Convergence has occurred and continues to occur between IFRS and U.S. GAAP. While many countries, including the United States, have made unilateral standard-level changes to converge their country-specific standards with IFRS, U.S. GAAP is the only set of standards with respect to which the IASB has made significant unilateral standard-level changes to IFRS. Also, U.S. GAAP is the only set of standards with which the IASB is willing to converge IFRS at the standard level in a multilateral way.

Some participants in the U.S. financial reporting supply chain still cling to the outdated belief that Convergence means other countries will discard their own financial reporting standards in favor of U.S. GAAP. But the reality is that more than 112 countries around the world have explicitly rejected set- and standard-level Convergence with U.S. GAAP in favor of set-level and unilateral standard-level Convergence with IFRS. This reality comes as a surprise to many people in the United States. For decades, U.S. GAAP was universally recognized as the most complete, highest-quality set of accounting standards in the world. Consequently, many observers believed that U.S. GAAP would be the focal point of Convergence. But U.S. GAAP has been slow to evolve and improve as the business world has become increasingly complex and global, and so it became possible for alternative, country-neutral standards to emerge and overshadow U.S. GAAP. It is now very clear that U.S. GAAP will *not* be the focal point of Convergence.

Another common misconception about Convergence in the United States is that giving companies their choice of using current U.S. GAAP or current IFRS is the goal of Convergence. But nothing could be further from the truth. Convergence is ultimately about all companies in all countries using the same set of country-neutral financial reporting standards. Although the SEC and other parties in the U.S. financial reporting supply chain have been increasingly willing to accept financial reports prepared in accordance with either current U.S. GAAP or current IFRS, such a choice does not constitute Convergence. However, there are some very significant implications of U.S. companies being able to choose which set of standards they will use, and those implications will be addressed in Chapter 20.

Yet another example of wrong thinking about Convergence stems from misinterpretations of the word *international* (the "I word" in IFRS, IASB, etc.). Many people in the United States incorrectly think that *international* is synonymous with *foreign,* and are prejudicially opposed to the idea of substituting "foreign" standards for U.S. standards, especially since many of those same people think that *foreign* is synonymous with *inferior.* Other people in the United States misperceive the point of converging U.S. GAAP with "international" standards based on the erroneous belief that such standards would apply only to multinational enterprises or those engaging in cross-border transactions, which is simply not the case. It is truly unfortunate, then, that the "I word" crops up so often in discussions of Convergence. It is helpful to think of Convergence not as focusing on *international* standards as much as on *global* standards. The word *global* implies *pervasiveness, uniformity,* and *country neutrality*—attributes that collectively constitute the essence of the goal of Convergence. To avoid potential misinterpretations, you can expect to see the word *global* in this book far more often than the word *international.*

To summarize, here are three main points to remember about Convergence from a U.S. perspective:

1. Convergence is *not* about what U.S. GAAP or IFRS are today, how those sets of standards currently differ from each other, or the opportunities that companies may have to choose between the two. Convergence is about what both U.S. GAAP and IFRS are *becoming.* And what they are becoming is a single set of higher-quality standards that companies in all countries will use.
2. U.S. GAAP has already changed in significant ways as a result of unilateral standard-level Convergence with IFRS. And IFRS has changed significantly as a result of unilateral standard-level Convergence with U.S. GAAP. Going forward, both U.S. GAAP and IFRS will change in profound ways as they converge with each other multilaterally at the standard level.
3. As a result of future multilateral standard-level Convergence between U.S. GAAP and IFRS, the global standards that we will end up with will *not* simply be cobbled together from the individual standards that exist now in U.S. GAAP and IFRS. Rather, future global standards will be substantially *better* than existing U.S. GAAP and IFRS. Why? It is difficult for the FASB or the IASB to justify changing their standards simply for the sake of Convergence, but both boards view changing to improved standards as highly desirable and consistent with their existing mandate to continuously improve their standards. So even though Convergence, per se, does not necessarily imply improvement, improvement will be inseparable from Convergence in practice.

Now that you know what Convergence is—and is not—you may be wondering "*Why* is Convergence happening?" The short answer is "Because it makes economic sense." A slightly longer, but definitely more enlightening answer about the causes of Convergence can be found in the next section.

What Is Causing Convergence?

Recall that existence and enforcement of financial reporting standards are the result of economic decisions made by end users of financial reports and by institutions that act on behalf of those end users. This implies that financial reporting standards will change if economic decisions about those standards that are made by or on behalf of end users change. And that is the fundamental cause of Convergence: the economic decisions that financial report users around the world are making with respect to financial reporting standards are different from the decisions that users have made in the past, and those different economic decisions are causing financial reporting standards around the world to become different from what they have been in the past.

In a nutshell, Convergence has happened and will continue to happen as the inescapable result of powerful economic forces within an increasingly globalized economy. But that does not mean that Convergence is some kind of sinister plot hatched by malevolent "foreign" powers bent on destroying our American financial reporting system. In fact, the strongest advocates of U.S. companies using a set of globally accepted standards in the future—standards that will be of higher quality than current U.S. GAAP—are found right here in the United States.

It was the United States that took the lead role in launching the modern Convergence movement in 1973, when it along with eight other countries formed the International Accounting Standards Committee (IASC), the predecessor to the IASB. (It is interesting to note that the FASB was not formed until *after* the IASC was formed). American institutions including the FASB, SEC, and the American Institute of Certified Public Accountants (AICPA) have all strongly supported true Convergence, that is, the adoption by companies in the United States and throughout the world of a single set of high-quality, country-neutral standards that would be superior in quality to current U.S. GAAP and current IFRS. Thus, Convergence is not the result of any attempt to forcibly replace U.S. financial reporting standards with "foreign" standards. Rather, it has arisen from the desire of investors, creditors, and other participants in capital markets to see companies in the United States and throughout the world eventually using a common set of standards that is better than any set that exists today.

It is no secret that the world's capital markets are becoming increasingly globalized. And so is the financial reporting supply chain. Investors, creditors, standard setters, and standard enforcers in the United States and throughout the world recognize that differences in financial reporting standards among countries make the global financial reporting supply chain less effective and less efficient than it would be if a single set of high-quality standards were used worldwide. In particular, the world's financial reporting standard setters, including the FASB, generally believe that the interests of investors, creditors, and the general public would be best served if all reporting entities throughout the world were to use the same set of high-quality, country-neutral financial reporting standards instead of the hodgepodge of country-specific standards that reporting entities use now.

The key chain of assumptions underlying that belief is as follows:

- The global use of a single set of high-quality, country-neutral standards would enhance the comparability of financial reports across all enterprises worldwide.
- The enhanced global comparability of financial reports would make capital markets throughout the world more efficient, that is, investors and creditors would be able to consider a much broader range of opportunities when making capital allocation decisions, which would in turn increase the likelihood of optimal capital allocation.
- Greater efficiency in the world's capital markets would (1) improve investors' and creditors' returns; (2) make our economy as a whole more efficient at satisfying people's needs and wants; and (3) stimulate greater investment in enterprises as a result of lowering costs of capital at all levels of risk. And greater investment in enterprises would stimulate economic growth, which would in turn result in further widespread economic benefits such as job creation.

Reporting entities themselves also have economic reasons to support converged financial reporting standards. For example, multinational enterprises would be able to reduce their costs of accounting and reporting if they were able to use a single set of standards across all business units, regardless of where in the world those business units were located. Even small, privately held domestic firms would enjoy both cost-savings opportunities and expansion opportunities as a result of the universal availability of financial reporting talent trained in globally accepted, country-neutral standards.

Conclusion

In ten years' time, companies in the United States and throughout the world will be using a set of high-quality financial reporting standards that will be unlike any set of financial reporting standards in use today. The financial reporting standards that U.S. companies will use in the future will not be U.S. GAAP. Nor will U.S. companies use IFRS as we know them today or any other existing set of standards. Rather, global standards of the future will be what current U.S. GAAP and IFRS are converging into.

While achieving the goal of Convergence—a single set of high-quality, global financial reporting standards—will result in economic benefits on a global scale, the process of Convergence will impose costs and challenges on all participants in the financial reporting supply chain. This book is meant to help you deal with the personal and managerial challenges of Convergence, and Chapter 2 will introduce you to the many ways in which Convergence will impact corporate financial reporting in the United States.

Notes

1. Norman Lyle, *Financial Reporting Supply Chain: Current Perspectives and Directions*. New York: International Federation of Accountants, 2008.
2. Financial Accounting Standards Board, Statement of Financial Accounting Concepts No. 1, *Objectives of Financial Reporting by Business Enterprises*, 1978.

CHAPTER 2

How Convergence Will Impact the United States

The global convergence of financial reporting standards began more than 35 years ago. In recent years, Convergence has resulted in significant changes to corporate financial reporting around the world. Those changes have had a profound impact on countries, companies, and individuals.

So far, the United States has felt the impact of Convergence only to a small degree. But Convergence has now reached a "tipping point" in the United States due to bold actions recently taken by the Financial Accounting Standards Board (FASB) and the Securities and Exchange Commission (SEC). Over the next decade, the impact of Convergence on the United States will grow steadily in magnitude—so much so that it would be difficult to overstate the long-term impact of Convergence.

It is important to recognize that every entity currently preparing financial reports in accordance with U.S. generally accepted accounting principles (GAAP) will be heavily affected by Convergence. Consequently, managers who are responsible for financial reporting in accordance with U.S. GAAP—whether for large or small companies, public or private, for-profit or not-for-profit—will find themselves facing many challenges in the years ahead.

To begin preparing for those challenges, you must first understand exactly how Convergence will impact your company, your department, and your career. This chapter will summarize the direct and indirect effects of Convergence on the United States and equip you with the basic understanding that you will need; Parts Two and Three of this book will provide additional detail.

Direct Effects of Convergence

The direct effects of Convergence on the United States can be summarized succinctly:

- U.S. GAAP is changing.
- U.S. GAAP is becoming optional.
- U.S. GAAP will eventually go away.

These direct effects will now be examined further.

Changes to Individual Standards in GAAP

The individual standards that constitute U.S. GAAP have changed and will continue to change significantly as a direct result of Convergence. Accounting for business combinations and employee stock options are two prominent examples of standards within U.S. GAAP that have recently undergone significant, unilateral change so as to converge with International Financial Reporting Standards (IFRS). And even bigger, multilateral changes are going to come at an accelerating pace in the near future. For example, the FASB and the International Accounting Standards Board (IASB) are working on a complete overhaul of the standard financial statements. As a result of the boards' joint efforts, the contents and presentation formats of the balance sheet, income statement, and cash flow statement will soon be very different from what they are today under both U.S. GAAP and IFRS.

Change in the Nature of GAAP

As the individual standards of U.S. GAAP change, the fundamental nature of U.S. GAAP will change as well. Currently, U.S. GAAP contains thousands of highly prescriptive, "bright line" rules. But it is the desire of the FASB, as part of its efforts to converge U.S. GAAP with IFRS, to transform U.S. GAAP from a rule-laden body of guidance into one that contains far fewer rules.

U.S. GAAP is often criticized for not being "principles based." In reality, U.S. GAAP is very principles based; it is just that GAAP's general principles have been almost completely overshadowed by its many specific rules.

And so, going forward, the FASB is attempting to both avoid introducing new rules-based standards and "thin out" rules in existing standards, which will shift U.S. GAAP away from being the unwieldy jumble of rules that we know today. Future GAAP will increasingly allow robust principles to stand on their own without the dubious benefit of numerous additional rules.

The FASB's shift away from rules-based guidance in U.S. GAAP is entirely consistent with the IASB's vision for IFRS, both now and in the future.

Although there are many rules in IFRS, there are significantly fewer rules than in U.S. GAAP. And IFRS, like U.S. GAAP, will purposely become even less rule laden over time.

U.S. financial professionals will be challenged to exercise professional judgment to a greater degree when applying standards that have fewer rules than what U.S. financial professionals are used to. See Chapter 5 for a more detailed discussion of principles-based standards and their implications.

GAAP Losing Its Exclusivity

Another major change to note is that, as a result of Convergence, U.S. GAAP is losing its "monopoly" as the exclusive basis for financial reporting in the United States. Recent actions of the SEC have effectively given certain publicly held entities under the SEC's jurisdiction the option to use either U.S. GAAP or IFRS as the basis for the financial reports that those entities must file with the SEC, and the SEC is expected to extend that option to more of the entities that it regulates. This dramatic shift in policy by the SEC is a clear signal that the SEC considers U.S. GAAP to be *sufficient, but not necessary,* to protect the interests of U.S. investors. And participants in the U.S. financial reporting supply chain are beginning to realize that it does not make economic sense to be different if it is not necessary.

In the short term, Convergence is creating opportunities and incentives for both publicly and privately held companies operating in the United States to abandon U.S. GAAP in favor of IFRS. Although U.S. GAAP and IFRS will continue to evolve and converge with each other at the standard level, the widespread adoption of IFRS outside of the United States creates a compelling reason for U.S. companies to consider switching to IFRS prior to their eventual standard-level Convergence with U.S. GAAP. IFRS have already been adopted by more than 112 countries (including the countries of the European Union), and are likely to be adopted by about 50 more countries within the next five years (including Canada, Japan, China, and India). In short, IFRS will soon be used in an overwhelming majority of the world's roughly 200 countries.

It is important to understand that the rationale for considering a switch to IFRS is not simply that "everybody else is doing it." The valid rationale for considering a switch to IFRS is based on U.S. companies—and U.S. capital markets—maintaining their *competitiveness* in a world where:

- Companies in other countries that have adopted IFRS have already begun to enjoy competitive advantages over U.S. companies, resulting from enhanced access to low-cost capital[1] on a global scale as well as from lower operating costs (accounting costs, compliance costs, etc.).

- Capital markets in other countries that allow or require financial reporting in accordance with IFRS have already begun to enjoy competitive advantages over U.S. markets resulting from increased efficiency.

The competitiveness of U.S. companies and capital markets has been a concern at the national level[2] as well as at the local level.[3] Continuing to cling to U.S. GAAP will very quickly make the United States the "odd country out." If U.S. companies persist in going their own way with regard to financial reporting standards, U.S. companies will become increasingly isolated and increasingly disadvantaged relative to their foreign competitors.

Keep in mind that giving companies their choice of which financial reporting standards to use is not the goal of Convergence. But allowing companies to choose a set of financial reporting standards so as to avoid being at a competitive disadvantage is a legitimate reason for the SEC to consider such a move. And although privately held companies are in theory free to choose now, a shift by publicly held companies will lead to conditions in the financial reporting supply chain and in the accounting profession that will make it more practical for privately held companies to switch as well.

Should all U.S. companies switch to IFRS if given the choice? Not necessarily. Some U.S. companies would certainly switch from U.S. GAAP to IFRS in the short term. However, most U.S. companies will have the opportunity and incentive to continue to use U.S. GAAP for an indefinite number of years to come. The key is that each company should be prepared to perform its own subjective assessment of the costs and benefits of switching versus not switching.

Specific guidance on making a choice between current U.S. GAAP and current IFRS is provided in Chapter 20. But regardless of whether individual companies switch to IFRS or stick with U.S. GAAP in the short term, Convergence will require financial professionals in all companies to be prepared for a future of country-neutral standards.

GAAP Going Away

Perhaps the most significant change to U.S. GAAP that will result from Convergence is that U.S. GAAP as we know it will eventually cease to exist. For publicly held companies, the future is clear: U.S. GAAP will be replaced by a set of global financial reporting standards that will be very different from current U.S. GAAP. For privately held companies, there are three likely scenarios:

1. Privately held companies will use the same global standards as publicly held companies.

2. Privately held companies will have the option to use a version of global standards adapted specifically for privately held companies. *This would be (or be similar to) the private-entity variant of IFRS that the IASB has been working on.*

3. Privately held companies will have the option to use a "stripped down" version of U.S. GAAP. *If publicly held companies in the United States stop using U.S. GAAP, advocates of differential standards for privately held companies (e.g., the Private Company Financial Reporting Committee) would surely take advantage of the opportunity to transform what we now know as U.S. GAAP into a radically simpler, more cost-effective set of financial reporting standards that would no longer be biased toward the needs and capabilities of publicly held companies.*

The key point is this: Under each of the above scenarios, financial reporting standards for both publicly and privately held companies will be significantly different from current U.S. GAAP.

To summarize the direct effects of Convergence once again:

- U.S. GAAP is changing.
- U.S. GAAP is becoming optional.
- U.S. GAAP will eventually go away.

In Part Two, you will find detailed descriptions of many of the forthcoming Convergence-driven changes to both U.S. GAAP and IFRS. But now we turn to examine the indirect effects of Convergence, that is, what else you can expect to happen as the U.S. financial reporting supply chain reacts to the fundamental transformation of U.S. GAAP.

Indirect Effects of Convergence

As a result of Convergence, financial reporting in the United States is certain to be impacted in profound ways. You have now seen the specific ways in which Convergence has already begun to affect U.S. GAAP directly. But it is also important to recognize that the impact of Convergence will be far greater than simply doing debits and credits differently. Convergence will have indirect—but still profound—technical and managerial implications for the entire financial reporting supply chain. And those technical and managerial implications will in turn cascade into profound career implications for U.S. financial managers.

Consequences of "Choice"

By now you should know that allowing companies to choose between U.S. GAAP and IFRS is *not* what is meant by *Convergence*. But "choice" is one of the direct results of the Convergence process, and it will have its own indirect effects on the financial reporting supply chain.

As of the time this book was written, the SEC was considering allowing certain U.S. companies under its jurisdiction (generally referred to as *issuers*, as in "issuers of securities to the public") to prepare and file financial statements using either IFRS or U.S. GAAP.[4] Such a choice would be certain to affect every aspect of the financial reporting supply chain. The effects would be different for different participants of the supply chain; for example, companies that prepare financial statements would be affected differently from firms that audit or analyze financial statements. Also, the impact would come sooner for some individuals and companies than for others. But no supply chain participant would be spared the impact of such a dramatic change in the U.S. financial reporting environment.

In particular, the introduction of an IFRS filing option would bring new opportunities for publicly held U.S. companies to minimize their operating and capital costs. Such an option would also bring managerial, educational, and career challenges to individual financial professionals. Unfortunately, few U.S. financial professionals are currently prepared to handle those challenges.

For example, corporate executives would have to decide whether to continue using U.S. GAAP or switch to IFRS. However, most corporate executives in the United States have little or no knowledge of IFRS, so they will be challenged to accurately assess the costs and benefits of switching to IFRS if the SEC were to allow it. Also, accounting and financial reporting processes would have to be overhauled in any company that makes the switch, which in turn will have significant implications for the company's governance, risk, and compliance initiatives, not to mention talent sourcing and information technology.

Because many companies would ultimately realize net benefits from switching to IFRS if the SEC were to allow it, the demand for professionals who have IFRS skills would increase if companies were given the option. This would also result in career opportunities and earning power being redistributed among individual professionals in a manner similar to the impact of the Sarbanes-Oxley Act—the minority who have the newly demanded skills and experience will be able to "write their own ticket," whereas the majority who lack the skills will find themselves competing for the decreasing number of jobs in which those skills are not needed.

What is also significant is that this phenomenon would play out on a global scale. If companies are not able to find U.S. professionals who have the required skills, those companies could easily and effectively offshore work to the many financial professionals around the world who have the required skills as a result of the widespread adoption of IFRS outside of the United States. With the United States looking like it will be the "last to arrive at the IFRS party," U.S. financial professionals could end up paying a heavy price in terms of lost career opportunities.

Another significant dimension of this phenomenon is that a shift toward IFRS by publicly held companies will have a collateral impact on privately held companies. In the United States, anything that affects accounting or financial reporting for publicly held companies ultimately affects the entire accounting profession. While it is possible for the accounting profession in the United States to accommodate the use of multiple sets of financial reporting standards, it may not be able to do so very well or for very long.

Allowing U.S. issuers to prepare and file financial statements using IFRS would also have a major impact on the accounting profession's educational system, which encompasses college degree programs as well as continuing education for working professionals. Because the U.S. accounting education system has virtually ignored IFRS, it is therefore currently incapable of helping either students or experienced professionals address the challenges and opportunities that would accompany a shift toward the use of IFRS in this country. Even if a shift toward IFRS use were to occur, the educational system would be challenged by its lack of resources and agility to adapt in a timely manner. But regardless of its present ability to adapt, adaptation of the educational system to IFRS would be inevitable.

Professional associations would certainly have to adapt as well. The associations that would be best positioned to serve their members are those that are global in scope and that represent large and growing segments of the profession, for example, Financial Executives International (FEI) and the Institute of Management Accountants (IMA).

Since professional associations are currently a major source of continuing education for working professionals, it is highly likely that associations will be expected to carry a significant share of the burden of helping professionals acquire the knowledge, skills, and abilities that will be increasingly in demand. Forward-thinking associations have already started to do this. For example, in September 2007, FEI organized its first Global Financial Reporting Convergence Conference and followed up with a second conference in June 2008. And associations are using their online and print publications to feature Convergence-themed articles.[5]

Looking further ahead, short-term action by the SEC to allow U.S. issuers to file using IFRS must be viewed as increasing the likelihood that the SEC will require filings prepared under converged global standards in the long term. In fact, such a requirement has been advocated by the FASB[6] and the American Institute of Certified Public Accountants (AICPA).[7] Of course, any long-term move away from U.S. GAAP will necessitate a reexamination of the FASB's role as the U.S. accounting standard setter.

The ability of U.S. issuers to adopt IFRS would have a significant impact on U.S. capital markets. The chief benefit would be to make investment in U.S. companies more attractive to foreign sources of capital. Thus, the United States could expect to attract more foreign investment.

Is there any downside to "choice"? Some people believe that "choice" would eliminate the FASB and IASB's interest in achieving Convergence between U.S. GAAP and IFRS. But that is not likely to happen, because "choice" is not the goal of standard setters—Convergence is. And for that matter, getting U.S. GAAP and IFRS converged at the standard level with each set of standards remaining separate and distinct from the other is not the goal of standard setters either—global set-level Convergence on one high-quality set of standards is.

Keep in mind that many companies that currently use U.S. GAAP will *not* switch to IFRS in the short run, even if given the choice to do so. Most of the companies that *would* switch to IFRS in the short run are likely to be large, publicly held, multinational companies. Yet Convergence will still have a profound impact on other companies because of the fundamental changes to U.S. GAAP discussed earlier in this chapter.

Stakeholder Relationships

Convergence is about more than just technical changes in standards and business processes. It is also about fundamental changes in a reporting entity's relationships with internal and external stakeholders. Convergence is bringing new opportunities and incentives for companies to communicate more effectively and efficiently with investors, creditors, securities analysts, auditors, and employees. Of course, there are new challenges as well in communicating the impact and rationale for Convergence to internal and external stakeholders.

The global convergence of accounting standards is clearly going to require a significant amount of reeducation of everyone in the financial reporting supply chain. Ignorance will prove very costly to investors, creditors, securities analysts, auditors, and chief financial officers. Fortunately, Convergence presents companies with the opportunity to exercise leadership in educating users of financial reports. Companies that take advantage of the opportunity will find themselves having better relationships with users, which by itself can be a significant competitive advantage.

Upheaval in the U.S. Labor Market

Both "choice" and Convergence will have significant short- and long-term effects on the U.S. labor market for financial reporting talent. In the short term, there will be a spike in demand for the relatively few professionals who can shepherd financial reporting supply chain participants through the challenges that await them. But the long-term effect will be quite different.

Over the next ten years, Convergence will obsolesce the knowledge, skills, and abilities of financial professionals. It will also globalize and commoditize the accounting labor market as a result of eliminating country-specific differences in financial reporting standards. U.S. financial professionals will find themselves to be small fish in a big global pool of workers—all of whom will be qualified to compete against each other for jobs anywhere in the world, and most of whom will be willing to work for far less compensation than U.S. financial professionals now enjoy. This phenomenon, coupled with the increasing ease of offshoring accounting and financial reporting work, is a major threat to the continued employability of U.S. financial professionals.

The coming impact of Convergence on labor markets for financial reporting talent is described in detail in Part Three.

Who Wins? Who Loses?

Convergence will create winners and losers in the financial reporting supply chain. Who wins?

- Users of financial reports
- Entities that prepare financial reports
- Financial professionals who expand their knowledge, skills, and abilities so as to stay on top of converging standards

Who loses? Financial professionals who fail to prepare for the impact of Convergence. That much is crystal clear.

Conclusion

The ultimate impact of Convergence on the United States is an unavoidable, disruptive transition to a future financial reporting environment that will be very different from today's. And that future environment is likely to be characterized by ongoing change to a far greater degree than many of today's financial professionals are comfortable with.

There is much that we do not know at this time about the details of our journey toward Convergence. We do not know precisely what will happen, how, or when. We do not know who will do what during the transition. And we certainly do not know how much it will all cost.

What we *do* know is that Convergence has the potential to bring many economic benefits to the United States—but few companies and individuals are prepared to capture the maximum benefits from Convergence. Different individuals and companies will experience different benefits and costs, and potentially experience those benefits and costs in different time frames. We also know that the transition from current U.S. GAAP to converged financial reporting standards will not be easy, fast, or cheap. Again, companies and individuals in the U.S. financial reporting supply chain are poorly prepared to bear the costs and cope with the challenges that Convergence will impose on them.

In general, the transition to higher-quality global standards will require an unprecedented degree of agility on the part of companies and individuals in the financial reporting supply chain. Part Four will help you, your department, and your company become more agile in preparing for and responding to the challenges of Convergence. But there is still quite a bit more to know about Convergence, such as why it is essential for you to begin preparing for the impact of Convergence *now*. You will learn why in Chapter 3.

Notes

1. For recent research on the impact of IFRS adoption on the cost of equity capital, see Edward Lee, Martin Walker, and Hans B. Christensen, *Mandating IFRS: Its Impact on the Cost of Equity Capital in Europe*, London: Certified Accountants Educational Trust, 2008.
2. See, for example, Committee on Capital Markets Regulation, *The Competitive Position of the U.S. Public Equity Market,* available at www.capmktsreg.org.
3. See, for example, U.S. Senator Charles Schumer and New York City Mayor Michael Bloomberg, *Sustaining New York's and the US' Global Financial Services Leadership,* available at www.senate.gov/~schumer.
4. U.S. Securities and Exchange Commission, *Concept Release on Allowing U.S. Issuers to Prepare Financial Statements in Accordance with International Financial Reporting Standards,* 2007.
5. See, for example, the author's monthly "Financial Reporting" column in *Strategic Finance,* from July 2008 on; and Parveen P. Gupta, Cheryl Linthicum, and Thomas G. Noland, "The Road to IFRS," *Strategic Finance,* September 2007.
6. Robert E. Denham and Robert H. Herz, comment letter "FASB/FAF response to SEC releases," November 7, 2007, available at www.sec.gov/comments/s7-20-07/s72007-20.pdf.
7. Randy G. Fletchall and Barry C. Melancon, comment letter re: File No. S7-20-07, November 12, 2007, available at www.sec.gov/comments/s7-20-07/s72007-48.pdf.

CHAPTER 3

Prepare for the Impact of Convergence Now

The process of Convergence has been under way for decades, but significant progress toward the goal of Convergence was not made until the dawn of the twenty-first century. Since then, a set of high-quality, country-neutral financial reporting standards—International Financial Reporting Standards (IFRS)—has been developed and is now embraced by a large and growing number of countries. However, as described in Chapter 1, the United States has experienced and will continue to experience Convergence differently from other countries.

Unlike in other countries, the impact of Convergence on financial reporting within the United States has been minimal so far. Going forward, however, the impact will increase rapidly to a profound level. Chapter 2 described the direct effects that Convergence will have on U.S. generally accepted accounting principles (GAAP) as well as the indirect effects that Convergence will have on the U.S. financial reporting supply chain over the next decade.

This book cannot insulate you from the impact of Convergence, but it can help you prepare for the impact and thereby avoid being overwhelmed by the coming transformation of the U.S. financial reporting supply chain. Whereas later chapters will delve into the specifics of what you need to know and do in order to prepare for the impact of Convergence, this chapter will explain why preparing for the impact of Convergence is not something that you or your company can afford to postpone. In other words, this chapter will help you understand why you must begin preparing for the impact of Convergence *now*.

What's the Rush?

Some financial managers in the United States are in outright denial about the coming impact of Convergence, and therefore see no urgency in preparing for it. Other U.S. financial managers understand that Convergence will profoundly impact them but do not believe that the impact is imminent, and therefore do not view preparing for the impact as urgent. Perhaps the latter group is misled by the slow progress of Convergence to date, by the lack of a fixed timetable for Convergence in the United States, or by the fact that it will take many years for Convergence to fully play out in this country. But regardless of the reason, failure to recognize the urgency of preparing for the impact of Convergence places U.S. financial managers and their companies at risk. And the longer the delay in preparing for the impact of Convergence, the greater the risks.

Specifically, delaying your preparations for the impact of Convergence will give rise to three risks:

1. *Risk to your company's competitiveness.* Your company will be at a significant competitive disadvantage versus other companies that have already adopted country-neutral financial reporting standards.
2. *Risk to your department's productivity.* Your department will be forced to play "catch up," adding to an already heavy workload and stress level.
3. *Risk to your employability.* You will find it more challenging to remain employed and to compete effectively for the career opportunities that you want.

Thus, the stakes are high at all levels: financial managers who delay in preparing for the impact of Convergence risk hurting their companies, their departments, and their careers. What raises the stakes even further are three factors that will impede you, your department, and your company from making swift progress in your preparations once you commit to preparing for the impact of Convergence:

1. *A lack of information.* Relevant, reliable information about Convergence from a U.S. perspective is relatively scarce.
2. *A lack of time.* You and your departmental colleagues have little time to spend doing anything other than your present duties.
3. *A lack of agility.* You, your company, and your company's stakeholders are probably unaccustomed to implementing major changes in strategy and operations as quickly as Convergence will require.

The risks arising from delays in preparing for the impact of Convergence and the factors that will impede your progress together have a clear implication: the time to begin preparing for the impact of Convergence is now. The longer you wait, the more likely the risks are to result in adverse consequences for you, your department, and your company. And the longer you wait, the less likely it is that you will be able to make up for lost time.

The following sections will provide additional details on the adverse consequences that are likely to arise from delays in preparing for the impact of Convergence and on the factors that will impede your progress once your preparations are under way.

Adverse Consequences of Waiting to Prepare

Each day of delay in preparing for the impact of Convergence increases the level of risk that you, your department, and your company face. As explained in the previous section, there are three specific risks that arise from delays in preparing for the impact of Convergence. All of those risks carry the possibility of adverse consequences, and each risk will now be examined in turn.

At Risk: Your Company's Competitiveness

Companies that avoid preparing for the impact of Convergence will soon find themselves to be at a disadvantage relative to their competitors. This is because companies that have already adopted current IFRS or are already preparing to adopt future global financial reporting standards are positioned to reduce their capital costs and operating costs sooner rather than later. (This aspect of Convergence is explained further in Chapter 20.) And any period of time during which your company's competitors are able to enjoy the advantage of lower capital costs and/or operating costs represents an opportunity for those competitors to build up a lead that your company may not be able to overcome. Thus, the sooner you prepare your company to use country-neutral standards, whether current IFRS or the future global standards that U.S. GAAP and IFRS are evolving into, the smaller the window of opportunity your company's competitors will have to exploit your lack of preparation.

Ultimately, planning to stick with country-specific financial reporting standards like current U.S. GAAP makes about as much sense (and stands about as much a chance of succeeding) as sticking with DOS after the rest of the world has already switched to Windows.

At Risk: Your Department's Productivity

To gauge the coming impact of Convergence on your department's work-load, it may be helpful to compare the impact of Convergence to the impact of the Sarbanes-Oxley Act of 2002 (SOX). The impact of Convergence will

be comparable to the impact of SOX in magnitude, as it will require fundamental changes in financial business processes and stakeholder communications. But the impact of Convergence will be vastly broader in scope, as
it will affect companies throughout the world, both public and private, that
currently use country-specific financial reporting standards like U.S. GAAP.

If financial managers had known what they were in for at the time
SOX was enacted, many of them would have made very different managerial decisions for their departments. Those different decisions would have
spared finance departments a lot of costs, disruptions to operations, and
extra work.

Fortunately, unlike SOX, the implications of Convergence for financial
managers are highly predictable and are addressed by this book, so there
is not likely to be a "regret factor" if you use the guidance in this book to
begin preparing for the impact of Convergence now. Understanding and
planning for the Convergence-related challenges that your department will
face will enable you to avoid the kind of unproductive "thrashing around"
that accompanied most SOX implementations.

At Risk: Your Employability

To state it plainly, if you do not start preparing for the impact of Convergence
now, you will soon find it more challenging to remain employed and to
access the best career opportunities. The most significant career threat that
you will increasingly face if you choose to delay your preparations for
the impact of Convergence is that you will be viewed by employers as
lacking in the knowledge, skills, and abilities (KSAs) that financial managers
will be expected to have as Convergence accelerates in the United States
and around the world. You may also have trouble keeping your current
job because Convergence will eliminate a significant amount of non-value-
adding work the financial managers now perform. And you could lose your
job if your company goes out of business as a result of experiencing higher
operating and capital costs than competitors who have adopted country-
neutral financial reporting standards.

In the short run, Convergence will redistribute personal earning power
and career opportunities among financial professionals in much the same
way that SOX did. Many financial managers look back on the early days
of SOX and wish they had made different—and more lucrative—career
decisions during that time. Fortunately, that does not have to happen again
with regard to Convergence.

In the long run, Convergence will transform labor markets for financial reporting talent around the world. Local markets for financial reporting talent will become increasingly globalized and commoditized as financial reporting standards converge. As a result, the emerging global labor

market for financial reporting talent will become hypercompetitive—and many workers in that market will be willing, able, and available to do your job for less compensation. See Part Three for more details on the profound—but often overlooked—impact that Convergence will have on labor markets.

Keep in mind that millions of financial professionals around the world already have a head start in working with country-neutral standards and acquiring the KSAs needed for career success in a world of rapidly converging financial reporting standards. And remember that you will soon be competing against them for jobs, with the disadvantage of "arriving late to the party." If you have more than ten years left before you expect to retire, the job you will retire from probably does not even exist today. It will certainly require different KSAs from your current job, and you will certainly face heavy competition to get and keep it.

Impeding Factors

As mentioned earlier in this chapter, your progress in preparing for Convergence in a timely manner is likely to be impeded by three specific factors. Each of the three factors—lack of information, lack of time, and lack of agility—will now be examined.

Lack of Information

To date, there has been relatively little relevant, reliable information available to help U.S. financial managers prepare for the impact of Convergence. And what little information exists is mainly focused on describing the technical differences between current U.S. GAAP and current IFRS. But emphasizing the current technical differences between those two sets of standards provides a narrow and misleading view of Convergence, and fails to address the broader educational needs of U.S. financial managers. As stated in Chapter 1, Convergence is *not* about what U.S. GAAP or IFRS are today or how those sets of standards currently differ from each other. Few participants in the U.S. financial reporting supply chain understand that they should be more interested in what U.S. GAAP and IFRS are *becoming* rather than what U.S. GAAP and IFRS *are*.

Of course, this book is an attempt to overcome the lack of useful information about preparing for the impact of Convergence. In particular, Part Two explains how both U.S. GAAP and IFRS are changing as they converge. But this book by itself cannot overcome the misplaced emphasis by many audit firms and other intermediaries in the financial reporting supply chain on the differences between current U.S. GAAP and current

IFRS. Until there is greater awareness of the scope of the challenges that Convergence is bringing to financial managers in the United States, a lack of useful information will continue to impede the progress of many.

Lack of Time

Preparing for the impact of Convergence will take a significant amount of effort—typically, the equivalent of a few months of full-time work. But U.S. financial managers have little "spare time" to devote to anything other than their current duties. And if you continue to be employed as a financial manager, you are not likely to have more spare time in the future to devote to preparing for Convergence than you do now. So if, like most managers, you can find only an hour or two each week to devote to preparing for the impact of Convergence, your preparations will literally take *years* of elapsed time.

Unfortunately, the point in time by which individuals and companies will need to complete their preparations is imminent and getting closer every day. But fortunately, your preparations do not have to be 100 percent complete in order for you, your department, and your company to experience benefits. The more you do and the sooner you do it, the better off you will be.

Lack of Agility

Time and time again, U.S. businesses have demonstrated a remarkable inability to handle change effectively and efficiently. But this does not reflect only the shortcomings of individuals; in the case of the U.S. financial reporting supply chain, most processes within the supply chain are predicated on a high degree of stability, including a high degree of stability in financial reporting standards. And because no one party is "in charge of" the entire supply chain, change is a formidable challenge for all of the supply chain's participants.

Unfortunately, never before has the incapacity for change been a bigger threat to U.S. financial managers and their companies. Individuals' and companies' success in a world of globally converged financial reporting standards depends on the degree to which they, along with the financial reporting supply chain as a whole, exhibit agility in anticipating and responding to changes in current standards. In this regard, the United States has begun to lag significantly behind other nations. The future relevance of U.S. companies within our increasingly global economy hinges in a very real way on our ability to overcome our inertia in the realm of financial reporting.

Conclusion

Financial managers in the United States are largely unprepared for the disruptive changes in the U.S. financial reporting environment that will soon occur as a result of Convergence. Does that mean we should attempt to slow down the wheels of progress? Bury our heads in the sand? Rail against the inevitable?

No. What it means is that we should accept the need to start preparing for the impact of Convergence right away. For corporate financial managers, there are critical managerial and career decisions that you will need to make now as U.S. GAAP and IFRS converge. Even though the full impact of Convergence on U.S. companies will not be felt for years, the impact will grow quickly to a level that will overwhelm the unprepared. Each day you delay your preparations increases the risks described in this chapter. And the longer you wait to prepare, the more likely it is that you will end up waiting too long.

Part I Epilogue

You should realize by now that while you cannot avoid the disruptive changes that Convergence is bringing to the U.S. financial reporting supply chain, you *can* take positive steps to manage the impact of those changes on your company, your department, and your career. Parts Two and Three describe the impact of those changes in detail, and Part Four will give you the practical guidance that you will need in order to manage the impact.

> *"The debate or question should no longer be whether we move to convergence of high-quality accounting standards, but how soon we can accomplish convergence.... Is there still hard work to be done towards convergence? Yes. Will there be bumps in the road as we take this journey? Absolutely. But it is a journey that must be taken."*
>
> —AICPA Vice President Charles E. Landes[1]

Note

1. Charles E. Landes, testimony provided to the Securities, Insurance, and Investment Subcommittee of the U.S. Senate Committee on Banking, Housing and Urban Affairs, at the Subcommittee's hearing on "International Accounting Standards: Opportunities, Challenges, and Global Convergence Issues," Washington, DC, October 24, 2007.

PART II

Impact of Convergence on Financial Reporting in the United States

Part Two examines in detail how Convergence will impact financial reporting in the United States. Recall from Chapter 2 that the direct effects of Convergence on U.S. generally accepted accounting principles (GAAP) can be summarized as follows:

- U.S. GAAP is changing.
- U.S. GAAP is becoming optional.
- U.S. GAAP will eventually go away.

To explore those direct effects further, each of the next ten chapters addresses a different aspect of financial reporting standards and describes:

- Recent Convergence-related changes to U.S. GAAP and International Financial Reporting Standards (IFRS)
- The current similarities and differences between U.S. GAAP and IFRS
- How U.S. GAAP and IFRS will change in the future as they converge into a single set of higher-quality, country-neutral standards

It is no exaggeration to say that virtually every aspect of preparing financial reports under both U.S. GAAP and IFRS will change as a result of Convergence. While the current similarities and differences between U.S. GAAP and IFRS are important to companies that are considering switching from U.S. GAAP to IFRS in the short term, all companies should recognize that both U.S. GAAP and IFRS will change profoundly over the long term. In fact, global financial reporting standards of the future will differ from current U.S. GAAP and IFRS to a much greater degree than U.S. GAAP and IFRS currently differ from each other.

Why will U.S. GAAP and IFRS change so much as they converge? It is tempting to think that the Financial Accounting Standards Board (FASB) and the International Accounting Standards Board (IASB) could eliminate the current differences between their respective sets of standards simply by choosing individual standards from one set or the other. The boards have actually done so to a limited extent in the past. However, both the FASB and the IASB have had long-standing, aggressive agendas for improving their standards. Many years ago, the boards realized that their improvement projects had to be coordinated if Convergence was ever going to be achieved. Although neither board has been willing to compromise on the quality of their current standards for the sake of Convergence, both boards have been eager to converge on standards that are better than current standards. So, from the boards' perspective, the improvement and Convergence of standards are inseparable. And because both U.S. GAAP and IFRS each have so much potential for improvement, Convergence between the two sets of standards will be characterized by major changes rather than minor ones, as described here in Part Two.

CHAPTER 4

Conceptual Frameworks

This chapter focuses on how Convergence is impacting the *conceptual frameworks* that underlie U.S. GAAP and IFRS. A conceptual framework for a set of financial reporting standards states the fundamental concepts on which that set of standards is based. It is similar to a constitution for a system of government, in the sense that a constitution states the fundamental concepts on which the system of government is based.

The concepts in a conceptual framework are general in nature and broad in scope. They typically include:

- The objective of financial reporting
- The kinds of financial statements that are to be prepared (balance sheet, income statement, etc.)
- The basic elements of financial statements (assets, liabilities, income, expenses, etc.)
- Desirable qualitative characteristics of the information in the financial statements (i.e., the nonquantitative characteristics of financial information that affect how useful the information is for making the kinds of economic decisions that users of financial statements make)
- Key assumptions (e.g., the relative stability of the purchasing power of the reporting currency)
- Key constraints (e.g., costs not to exceed benefits)

There are many advantages in having a conceptual framework to serve as the foundation for a set of financial reporting standards. Having a conceptual framework helps to ensure that:

- Time and effort are not wasted reestablishing basic concepts each time an individual financial reporting standard is developed.
- Developed standards are consistent with explicitly recognized assumptions and constraints.

- Developed standards are consistent with each other.
- The objective of financial reporting is attained.

Because conceptual frameworks are so fundamental to the standards that are based on them, convergence of conceptual frameworks is necessary for the convergence of standards themselves. If different standard setters disagree on the basic concepts of financial reporting, then it is unlikely that those standard setters will ever agree on specific standards. Fortunately, the FASB and IASB both recognize that converging their respective conceptual frameworks is essential to converging U.S. GAAP and IFRS.

Comparison of Conceptual Frameworks

U.S. GAAP and IFRS were developed from different conceptual frameworks. This section introduces the two conceptual frameworks and broadly summarizes the current similarities and differences between them.

The conceptual framework for U.S. GAAP is documented in a series of *Statements of Financial Accounting Concepts* issued by the FASB between 1978 and 2000. In the U.S. GAAP conceptual framework, the main objective of financial reporting is to "provide information that is useful to present and potential investors and creditors and other users in making rational investment, credit, and similar decisions."[1]

The conceptual framework for IFRS is documented in the *Framework for the Preparation and Presentation of Financial Statements*, which was issued by the IASB in 2001. In the IFRS conceptual framework, the objective of financial statements is to "provide information about the financial position, performance, and changes in financial position of an entity that is useful to a wide range of users in making economic decisions."[2]

There are currently many similarities between the FASB's and IASB's conceptual frameworks. In particular, the overall objectives of financial reporting are similar, as noted above. Also, the kinds of financial statements that are to be prepared for a reporting period are similar between the conceptual frameworks. There are additional similarities in the key assumptions and key constraints that apply to financial reporting under each framework. And both frameworks rely on similar concepts of capital maintenance for distinguishing returns *on* capital from returns *of* capital.

But while there are many similarities between the FASB's and IASB's conceptual frameworks, there are also some significant differences. Each conceptual framework emphasizes certain qualitative characteristics and certain aspects of those qualitative characteristics differently from the other conceptual framework. Also, the set of financial statement elements in the FASB's conceptual framework is more comprehensive than that in the

IASB's conceptual framework, and some of the individual elements that are common to both frameworks are defined differently.

FASB-IASB Joint Conceptual Framework Project

Both the FASB and IASB see achieving the long-term goal of Convergence as dependent on the development of a single conceptual framework on which future financial reporting standards will be based. Since October 2004, the boards have been working together on what they describe as an "improved common conceptual framework" that will bring together and improve upon both boards' current frameworks. Because U.S. GAAP and IFRS cannot fully converge unless the fundamental concepts on which those sets of standards are based converge, the FASB-IASB joint conceptual framework project is truly critical to the success of Convergence.

Note that the objective of the joint conceptual framework project is *not* to have two separate frameworks that happen to be the same as each other. It is about having a single, common framework that will underlie a single, globally converged set of financial reporting standards in the future. In other words, the project is about converging the conceptual frameworks on which U.S. GAAP and IFRS are based in order to facilitate the Convergence of U.S. GAAP and IFRS themselves.

Changes to conceptual frameworks are infrequent. Neither the FASB nor the IASB is inclined to tinker incrementally with their existing frameworks. As a result, neither the FASB nor the IASB's conceptual framework has changed in many years, and the impact of the conceptual framework project will likely not be felt for many years to come. However, the FASB and IASB do *not* view the completion of the conceptual framework project as a necessary predecessor to other progress on Convergence. Thus, the conceptual framework project is being conducted in parallel with many other joint projects focused on the Convergence of individual standards between U.S. GAAP and IFRS.

As is appropriate for a long-term, complex undertaking, the conceptual framework project has been divided into phases. The following phases are currently active and are being conducted simultaneously:

- Phase A: Objective and Qualitative Characteristics
- Phase B: Elements and Recognition
- Phase C: Measurement
- Phase D: Reporting Entity

The status of each of the active phases is summarized below. Subsequent phases will address other issues, such as presentation and disclosure.

Phase A: Objective and Qualitative Characteristics

To date, the boards' joint work in Phase A of the project has resulted in drafts of the first two chapters of an enhanced conceptual framework. The draft chapters define the objective of financial reporting by private-sector business entities and the qualitative characteristics of decision-useful financial reporting information.

In July 2006, the FASB and the IASB each published for public comment a consultative document setting out their preliminary views on the draft chapters. The public comment period for those documents ended in November 2006. In subsequent redeliberations, the boards made minor revisions to their preliminary views and published an exposure draft (ED) of the chapters in May 2008. The comment period for the ED ended on September 29, 2008.

Currently, the boards' proposed objective of general-purpose financial reporting is "to provide financial information about the reporting entity that is useful to present and potential equity investors, lenders, and other creditors in making decisions in their capacity as capital providers."[3] That objective is generally consistent with the objectives stated in the FASB's and IASB's existing conceptual frameworks.

The boards have identified *relevance* and *faithful representation* as the two *necessary* qualitative characteristics of financial reporting information (i.e., those characteristics must be present in order for financial reporting information to be decision useful). In addition, *comparability*, *verifiability*, *timeliness*, and *understandability* were identified as being *desirable* qualitative characteristics that complement the necessary characteristics and enhance decision usefulness when they are present.[4] On the whole, the set of qualitative characteristics currently proposed by the boards represents a blending of the qualitative characteristics and other concepts from both existing conceptual frameworks.

Phase B: Elements and Recognition

Some of the most dramatic developments in the conceptual framework project are occurring in Phase B. Consider the following working definition that the boards have developed: "An *asset* of an entity is a present economic resource to which the entity has a right or other access that others do not have."[5] Contrast that definition of an asset to the one found in the existing U.S. GAAP conceptual framework: "Assets are probable future economic benefits obtained or controlled by a particular entity as a result of past transactions or events."[6] Even though the definitions of an asset in the existing U.S. GAAP and IFRS frameworks are similar to each other, the boards have chosen to discard traditional concepts on which those existing definitions are based (such as probable future economic benefits, control, and past transactions or events) in developing a new working definition of an asset for the common conceptual framework.

Now consider the boards' working definition of a liability: "A *liability* of an entity is a present economic obligation for which the entity is the obligor."[7] And once more, contrast that definition with its counterpart in the current U.S. GAAP conceptual framework: "Liabilities are probable future sacrifices of economic benefits arising from present obligations of a particular entity to transfer assets or provide services to other entities in the future as a result of past transactions or events."[8] Again, long-standing concepts of probability, economic benefits, the future, and the past have been deliberately discarded by the boards.

The working definitions of assets and liabilities that have come out of Phase B of the conceptual framework project so far represent radical departures from the definitions of those elements found in the current FASB and IASB conceptual frameworks. But those are just two examples of how far the boards are willing to go in making changes to both U.S. GAAP and IFRS that they believe will improve their respective sets of standards as the boards eliminate differences between the sets. So as much as any Convergence effort under way today, this phase of the conceptual framework project illustrates multilateral Convergence in practice (i.e., the elimination of differences through mutual improvements).

There is much more work ahead in this phase, especially related to issues of determining the unit of account and concepts for recognition and derecognition, so we can expect more major changes to come.

Phase C: Measurement

The objective of Phase C of the joint conceptual framework project is to select a set of measurement bases that satisfy the objectives and qualitative characteristics of financial reporting. In early 2007, the FASB and IASB completed their deliberations on the first stage of this phase, which involved listing and defining measurement basis candidates. Starting with more than 50 measurement basis candidates, most of which were found in existing financial reporting standards, the boards narrowed the list down to the following nine:

1. Past entry price
2. Past exit price
3. Modified past amount
4. Current entry price
5. Current exit price
6. Current equilibrium price

7. Value in use
8. Future entry price
9. Future exit price

The boards concluded that all of these measurement bases were appropriate for use with both assets and liabilities, and provided two definitions for each candidate on the list—one from the perspective of an asset and one from the perspective of a liability.[9]

Note that *past entry price* is more commonly known as *historical cost*, which is the primary measurement basis for most assets and liabilities under U.S. GAAP today. However, under both U.S. GAAP and IFRS, the use of *current exit price* is becoming increasingly prevalent—and increasingly controversial. You may be familiar with that measurement basis by its more common name, *fair value*. (See Chapter 8 for a discussion of fair value and related measurement issues.)

The next step is for the boards to consider their staffs' initial evaluation of the measurement basis candidates. Later, the boards will consider issues related to selecting measurement bases for use in financial statements, with the goal of issuing a discussion paper describing their views on those issues.

Phase D: Reporting Entity

The objective of Phase D is to determine what constitutes a reporting entity for the purposes of financial reporting. In May 2008, the FASB and the IASB each published for public comment a consultative document setting out their preliminary views on the definition of a reporting entity. The comment period ended on September 29, 2008.

The boards have tentatively decided that a reporting entity should be broadly described as "a circumscribed area of business activity of interest to present and potential equity investors, lenders and other creditors in making decisions in their capacity as capital providers," without regard to whether the business activity is structured as a legal entity.[10]

Substantive issues to be considered throughout this phase include defining the composition of "group" entities (e.g., parent-subsidiary groups), the presentation of consolidated and/or separate financial statements for groups and their members, and the concept of control as being the factor that unifies a group of entities.

Conclusion

The global Convergence of financial reporting standards will require Convergence on a common conceptual framework for those standards. The

FASB and IASB are actively pursuing the development of a converged conceptual framework, and it is already clear that the converged framework will be different from existing frameworks in significant ways. To stay abreast of the boards' progress on their joint conceptual framework project, visit the project page at the FASB web site http://fasb.org/project/conceptual_framework.shtml.

Notes

1. Financial Accounting Standards Board, Statement of Financial Accounting Concepts No. 1, *Objectives of Financial Reporting by Business Enterprises*, paragraph 34, 1978.
2. International Accounting Standards Board, *Framework for the Preparation and Presentation of Financial Statements*, paragraph 12, 2001.
3. Financial Accounting Standards Board, Exposure Draft, *Conceptual Framework for Financial Reporting: The Objective of Financial Reporting and Qualitative Characteristics and Constraints of Decision-Useful Financial Reporting Information*, May 29, 2008.
4. Ibid.
5. Financial Accounting Standards Board, Project Update, "Conceptual Framework—Phase B: Elements and Recognition" [online], October 31, 2008 [accessed November 7, 2008], available at www.fasb.org/project/cf_phase-b.shtml.
6. Financial Accounting Standards Board, Statement of Financial Accounting Concepts No. 6, *Elements of Financial Statements*, paragraph 25, 1985.
7. See note 5.
8. Financial Accounting Standards Board, Statement of Financial Accounting Concepts No. 6, *Elements of Financial Statements*, paragraph 35, 1985.
9. Staff of the Financial Accounting Standards Board, "Conceptual Framework Project, Phase C: Measurement, Milestone I Summary Report—Inventory and Definitions of Possible Measurement Bases," available at www.fasb.org/project/CF_Milestone_I_Summary_Report.pdf.
10. Financial Accounting Standards Board, Preliminary Views, *Conceptual Framework for Financial Reporting: The Reporting Entity*, May 29, 2008.

CHAPTER 5

Principles-Based Standards

From a U.S. perspective, it is widely believed that the global Convergence of financial reporting standards will involve a shift away from *rules-based* standards toward *principles-based* standards. However, that perception of upcoming changes in the nature of financial reporting standards is not entirely accurate. To challenge common misunderstandings about principles-based standards and rules-based standards, this chapter will:

- Explain the differences between principles and rules.
- Accurately characterize, compare, and contrast the nature of standards in both U.S. generally accepted accounting principles (GAAP) and International Financial Reporting Standards (IFRS) today.
- Explore the impact of Convergence on the nature of standards in both U.S. GAAP and IFRS.

Ultimately, this chapter will clarify the role of principles-based standards in Convergence and, in turn, deepen your understanding of how Convergence will (and will not) impact financial reporting in the United States.

Principles versus Rules

Financial reporting standards can be very diverse in nature. A simplistic distinction between different kinds of standards is often made by characterizing individual standards as being either *principles* or *rules*. Before exploring the relevance of that distinction within the context of Convergence, it is useful to identify some of the key differences between principles and rules:

- Principles are general in nature, while rules are specific and detailed.
- Principles describe *what* should be done, whereas rules describe *how*.
- Principles tend to be few in number, while rules tend to be numerous.
- Compliance with principles tends to be a matter of degree rather than a yes-or-no distinction as in the case of rules.

A preponderance of either principles or rules in a given set of standards makes it possible for the set as a whole to be characterized as either *principles based* or *rules based*. Such characterizations are relevant to Convergence because the relative merits of principles versus rules are frequently debated by participants in the financial reporting supply chain who wish to see financial reporting standards improve as they converge.

Unfortunately, such debates often degenerate into confusing, unproductive arguments due to flawed thinking about the principles-based/rules-based characterization of sets of standards. Much of the popular debate about principles and rules in financial reporting standards presumes that *principles based* and *rules based* are mutually exclusive characterizations of a given set of standards, or are opposite poles of a continuum such that the more a given set of standards is principles based, the less it must be rules based, and vice versa.

However, it is much more accurate to think of *principles based* and *rules based* not as mutually exclusive alternatives, nor as opposite poles of a single continuum, but rather as two independent continua. In other words, the degree to which a set of standards is principles based should be recognized as being independent of the degree to which that set of standards is rules based. Recognizing that there are really two separate dimensions on which sets of financial reporting standards can be characterized will lead to more accurate characterizations of sets of standards. More accurate characterizations of sets of financial reporting standards with regard to each dimension will lead to more intelligent debate over the degree to which any future, converged set financial reporting standards should be principles based and the degree to which such a set should be rules based. And more intelligent debate will allow for the possibility that a single set of global standards could be—and maybe even should be—significantly principles based *and* significantly rules based.

U.S. GAAP versus IFRS: Where Are We Now?

Two myths that have pervaded and corrupted the debate about the roles of principles and rules in Convergence are that (1) current U.S. GAAP is not principles based; and (2) current IFRS are not rules based. Those myths are mischaracterizations that have arisen from the widespread failure to perceive *principles based* and *rules based* as independent dimensions, as described in the previous section.

The truth is that both current U.S. GAAP and current IFRS are principles based.[1] In fact, they are both based on very similar principles. It is also true that both current U.S. GAAP and current IFRS are rules based. Both sets of standards have numerous rules in addition to their principles. The key difference: there are many more rules in U.S. GAAP than there are in IFRS.

In order to converge U.S. GAAP and IFRS, the Financial Accounting Standards Board (FASB) and the International Accounting Standards Board (IASB) must eventually concur on the degree to which a converged set of standards should be principles based and the degree to which that set of standards should be rules based. To accurately predict how a converged set of financial reporting standards would or would not resemble current U.S. GAAP and current IFRS on those dimensions, it is necessary to accurately frame the central issue in the debate about principles and rules.

"Principles Alone" versus "Principles Plus Rules"

There is widespread agreement among preparers, auditors, and users of financial reports regarding the desirability of including principles in any set of standards used in the financial reporting supply chain. When principles are explicitly stated within a set of financial reporting standards, those principles help to make the standards more understandable and help to prevent inconsistencies and conflicts among individual standards. Thus, it is widely considered desirable for a set of financial reporting standards to be principles based.

The central issue on which participants in the financial reporting supply chain disagree is whether a set of financial reporting standards should consist solely of principles or whether a set of standards should contain rules in addition to principles (and if so, to what extent). Consequently, an accurate framing of the issue pits a *principles-alone* approach against a *principles-plus-rules* approach to standard setting. We turn now to examine the relative merits of each approach.

Principles-Alone Approach

The main argument in favor of a principles-alone approach is that a set of financial reporting standards composed solely of a relatively small number of general principles would be easier to develop, easier to understand, and easier to apply than if the set were to contain rules in addition to (or instead of) principles. This approach certainly has the potential for relieving financial professionals in the United States and around the world from *standards overload*—the result of a seemingly never-ending stream of new and different financial reporting standards, almost all of which are rules.[2]

Although the argument in favor of a principles-alone approach is compelling, there are many arguments against it. One is that relying on principles alone would result in overly simplistic accounting for inherently complex events and transactions, such as those involving derivative financial instruments. Other arguments against a principles-alone approach arise from the fact that principles alone offer no guidance on how they could be or should be interpreted and implemented in practice. Thus, a principles-alone approach would force redundant work on individual accountants and companies to "reinvent the wheel" countless times in determining how to apply each principle.

If there are no specific, "bright-line" application rules to augment the principles in a given set of standards, then it would certainly be more difficult for auditors and regulators to determine whether a preparer has complied "enough" with the principles in the preparation and presentation of financial statements. A lack of detailed guidance on interpreting and implementing principles would also expose "upstream" participants in the financial reporting supply chain to having their judgments second-guessed by regulators and by "downstream" participants, which would then lead to time-consuming, costly disagreements among preparers, auditors, and regulators—disagreements that would ultimately undermine the confidence of users in financial reports. And as BDO Seidman warns, "With minimal implementation guidance, . . . after-the-fact litigation about the economic substance of transactions will proliferate."[3]

Perhaps the most significant concern of standard setters, regulators, and financial report users is that the lack of detailed prescriptive guidance in a principles-alone set of standards would allow diversity in practice to flourish, and therefore could lead to noncomparability among financial reports, even when those reports are prepared in accordance with the same set of principles. That situation could also provide more opportunities for earnings management to occur. Those possibilities are especially troubling because a main motivation to pursue the goal of Convergence is the prospect of attaining greater comparability of financial information across entities The Institute of Chartered Accountants of Scotland has noted plainly that "the more comparability [is] required, the more rules have to be put in place to enforce it."[4]

Recall from Chapter 4 that both the FASB and IASB regard comparability as a highly desirable qualitative characteristic of financial information. It comes as no surprise, then, that the FASB has rejected "principles-only" standards, because such standards "could lead to situations in which professional judgments, made in good faith, result in different interpretations for similar transactions and events, raising concerns about comparability."[5] On this point, the Securities and Exchange Commission (SEC) staff concurs with the FASB: "The result of principles-only standards can be a significant loss of comparability among reporting entities."[6]

Principles-Plus-Rules Approach

The chief arguments for using a principles-plus-rules approach to setting financial reporting standards are:

- Rules are necessary to faithfully represent the economic substance of complex transactions and events.
- Rules minimize the redundant, non-value-adding work of both individual professionals and companies each figuring out for themselves how to apply principles.
- Rules help to eliminate diversity in practice and therefore enhance the comparability of financial information among entities.
- Rules enhance the auditability of financial information and enhance the enforceability of standards.
- Rules help preparers and auditors manage compliance risks and legal risks, especially in highly litigious jurisdictions like the United States.[7]

The chief argument against using a principles-plus-rules approach to financial reporting standards is that a set of financial reporting standards becomes more difficult to develop, understand, and apply the more the set is rules based. FASB Statement No. 133, *Accounting for Derivative Instruments and Hedging Activities*, is often cited as the most egregious example of "rules gone wrong." International Accounting Standard 39, *Financial Instruments: Recognition and Measurement*, has been similarly vilified, which is not surprising because it is based to a large extent on FASB Statement No. 133.

Rules-based standards have also been criticized for allowing the "engineering" of a transaction so as to produce a particular accounting treatment regardless of whether that accounting treatment accurately faithfully represents the economic substance of the transaction. As the SEC staff has pointed out: "[E]xperience demonstrates that rules-based standards often provide a roadmap to avoidance of the accounting objectives inherent in the standards. Internal inconsistencies, exceptions, and bright-line tests reward those willing to engineer their way around the intent of the standards. This can result in financial reporting that is not representationally faithful to the underlying economic substance of transactions and events. In a rules-based system, financial reporting may well come to be seen as an act of compliance rather than an act of communication. Moreover, it can create a cycle of ever-increasing complexity, as financial engineering and implementation guidance vie to keep up with one another."[8] As an example, FASB Statement No. 13, *Accounting for Leases*, has often been criticized for containing a plethora of rules that provide the motivation and means for companies to structure leasing transactions in a manner that keeps true economic liabilities off of the lessee's balance sheet.

But proponents of rules-based standards contend that the problem is not rules per se; it is when standard setting fails to incorporate rules appropriately into a set of principles-based standards. For example, problems occur when promulgated rules are not linked to principles or are linked to poor principles,[9] such as principles that:

- Are not consistent with the conceptual framework on which they should be based
- Conflict with each other
- Are unlikely, when applied, to result in the faithful representation of the economic substance of a transaction or event

Rules may also be problematic if they:

- Are not linked to principles at all
- Are not consistent with each other
- Impose arbitrary bright-line tests
- Allow too many alternative accounting treatments
- Represent special-interest exceptions to other rules

In this view, the solution to all of the problems associated with rules-based standards is "better" standard setting. But it is important to realize that the blame for the problems of rules-based standards cannot be pinned solely on standard setters, and it is therefore unfair to expect standard setters alone to fix those problems. In particular, the demand for rules in U.S. GAAP stems from rational behavior in a legal and regulatory environment that contains many disincentives for financial professionals who exercise professional judgment. IASB Chairman Sir David Tweedie explains:

> [T]he US approach is a product of the environment in which US standards are set. Simply put, US accounting standards are detailed and specific because the FASB's constituents have asked for detailed and specific standards. Companies want detailed guidance because those details eliminate uncertainties about how transactions should be structured. Auditors want specificity because those specific requirements limit the number of difficult disputes with clients and may provide a defence in litigation. Securities regulators want detailed guidance because those details are thought to be easier to enforce.[10]

The FASB itself has noted that "many preparers and auditors ... have been requesting detailed rules and bright lines in an apparent effort to reduce the need for the exercise of judgment in inherently subjective areas."[11]

Regardless of the influence of constituents on standard setters, good standard setting is simply more difficult the more rules based a set of standards is. So there is probably a level of rules in each set of standards that represents the optimal trade-off between the quantity and quality of rules. Ultimately, "[t]he highest quality standards are an artful blend of underlying principles and implementation guidance."[12] In any case, both the IASB and the FASB view the optimal level of rules as being lower than that of current IFRS and far lower than that of current U.S. GAAP.

Outlook for Converged Standards

Both the FASB and the IASB are under considerable pressure from their constituents to minimize the number of rules in financial reporting standards while at the same time ensuring that the application of those standards will result in financial statements that are representationally faithful, sufficiently comparable across entities, cost-effective to prepare and audit, and defensible in court. But most participants in the financial reporting supply chain will acknowledge that it is unrealistic to expect standard setters to produce a set of standards that satisfies all of those criteria. So what should we expect as the FASB and the IASB work to converge U.S. GAAP and IFRS into a single set of standards that will be at least as principles-based as each separate set of standards is now and that will also be rules-based to an optimal degree? This section will describe what financial-statement preparers can realistically expect regarding the nature of future financial reporting standards.

First and foremost, we can expect the FASB and the IASB to clearly articulate agreed-upon principles in converged standards. Principles will be much more explicitly stated in converged standards than they are now in U.S. GAAP. And those principles will be more discernibly linked to the improved, converged conceptual framework that the boards are working on. (Of course, if the boards fail to agree on the principles, they will have little chance of agreeing on anything else!)

Although the boards are inclined to allow robust principles to stand on their own without the dubious benefit of numerous additional rules, the boards are unlikely to go so far as to adopt a principles-alone approach to standard setting. From its perspective, the FASB:

> ... *believes that the amount of necessary guidance will vary depending on the nature and complexity of the arrangements that are the subject of the standard....[T]here should be enough guidance such that a principle is understandable, operational, and capable of being applied consistently in similar situations. Judgment is required to decide how much guidance is needed to achieve those objectives, without*

providing so much guidance that the overall standard combined with its implementation guidance becomes a collection of detailed rules. Therefore, the amount and nature of implementation guidance will vary from standard to standard.[13]

To the extent that converged standards will be rules based in addition to being principles based, the boards must agree on whether principles should take precedence over rules. It has been suggested that an obligatory *true-and-fair override* be incorporated into principles-plus-rules standards in order to appropriately resolve any inconsistencies between rules and principles.[14] In contrast, compliance with the detailed rules of U.S. GAAP today almost always takes precedence over consistency with U.S. GAAP's underlying principles, so the use of a true-and-fair override by reporting entities in the United States has been extremely rare.

In any case, the FASB and IASB will aim toward making future standards less rules based than U.S. GAAP and IFRS are now. That means that converged standards will generally contain less interpretation and implementation guidance. More specifically, converged standards will contain fewer:

- Explicitly described alternative accounting treatments
- Bright-line tests
- Exceptions
- Industry-specific rules
- "Safe harbors"
- "Anti-abuse" provisions

Reductions in rules relative to current U.S. GAAP are likely to be significant and pervasive, as current U.S. GAAP is widely perceived to contain too many rules in nearly every area. In contrast, because there are not as many rules in current IFRS as there are in current U.S. GAAP, the overall reduction in rules relative to current IFRS will be less dramatic.

While having fewer rules will not necessarily lead to insufficient comparability, having fewer rules will certainly lead to less comparability. This gives rise to a significant risk that any reductions in rules may be short lived. Standards will always be subject to the threat of "rules creep" over time, since "[a] principles-based standard often becomes a rules-based standard in an effort to increase comparability and consistency."[15] Going forward, it will be helpful for standard setters and their constituents to recognize that "complete comparability is never possible in accounting."[16]

"Backsliding" toward more rules is also a risk if disincentives to exercising professional judgment are not eliminated from the U.S. legal and regulatory environment. To the extent that the FASB and IASB succeed in making future standards less rules based than present-day standards, U.S.

preparers and auditors can expect to have to exercise professional judgment more frequently and in a more sophisticated manner than they do today. This will challenge financial professionals to learn to make the kinds of professional judgments that will be required in the absence of highly prescriptive financial reporting guidance. It will also challenge preparers and auditors to learn to respect each other's professional judgments. There is widespread acknowledgment among practitioners, however, that "generations of accountants and accounting teachers who were raised in a rules environment may find this a difficult adjustment to make."[17]

Thus, reductions in rules will lead to preparers and auditors to push for major changes in the legal and regulatory environment in which the U.S. financial reporting supply chain operates. Failure to bring about change in the U.S. legal and regulatory environment could easily result in increased pressure on standard setters to restore the level of prescriptive guidance in converged standards to that of current U.S. GAAP, or at least that of current IFRS. Depending on what does or does not happen *outside* the standard-setting arena in the long run, it is possible that we might end up right back where we started. "The accounting culture in the United States is one of highly specific and prescriptive standards, and a change in culture is not simple to achieve."[18]

Conclusion

Going forward, the FASB and IASB will undoubtedly endeavor to bolster the role of principles in converged standards. The boards will also attempt to "thin out" rules in existing standards as well as avoid introducing new rules-based standards. But the success of those efforts will be effectively dictated by the pace and degree of:

- Change in country-specific regulatory and legal disincentives that discourage preparers and auditors from exercising professional judgment to the extent required in the absence of detailed prescriptive guidance
- Further reforms of intra-entity governance of the financial reporting function

Ultimately, the prospects for future financial reporting standards to be less rules based depend on whether an atmosphere of trust prevails throughout the financial reporting supply chain. Preparers must be willing and able to earn the trust of downstream supply chain participants by consistently telling the truth in a truthful manner. Downstream participants and regulators must be willing to accept that different judgments can and will be made by different professionals in the supply chain without necessarily undermining the usefulness of financial reporting.

Notes

1. See Katherine Schipper, "Principles-Based Accounting Standards," *Accounting Horizons*, Vol. 17, No. 1, March 2003.
2. "The term 'standards overload' is one that has been used off and on over the years by the FASB's various constituent groups to describe their concerns about not only the volume of accounting rules and the level of complexity and detail of those rules, but also the resulting profusion of footnote disclosures and the difficulty of finding all the accounting rules on a particular subject." Financial Accounting Standards Board, "The FASB Addresses Standards Overload through New Projects," *FASB Report*, February 28, 2002.
3. BDO Seidman, LLP, Comment letter on proposal of the Financial Accounting Standards Board, "Principles-Based Approach to U.S. Standard Setting," December 2, 2002.
4. The Institute of Chartered Accountants of Scotland, *Principles Not Rules: A Question of Judgement*, April 2006.
5. Financial Accounting Standards Board, *Principles-Based Approach to U.S. Standard Setting*, October 21, 2002.
6. Staff of the U.S. Securities and Exchange Commission, *Study Pursuant to Section 108(d) of the Sarbanes-Oxley Act of 2002 on the Adoption by the United States Financial Reporting System of a Principles-Based Accounting System*, July 25, 2003.
7. "Detailed rules and authoritative guidance . . . serve standard setters' and regulators' objective of reducing the opportunities of managers to use judgments to manage earnings (and of auditors to have to accept that practice)." George J. Benston, Michael Bromwich, and Alfred Wagenhofer, "Principles- versus Rules-Based Accounting Standards: The FASB's Standard Setting Strategy," *Abacus*, Vol. 42, No. 2, 2006.
8. See note 6.
9. See Christopher W. Nobes, "Rules-Based Standards and the Lack of Principles in Accounting," *Accounting Horizons*, Vol. 19, No. 1, March 2005.
10. Statement of Sir David Tweedie before the Committee on Banking, Housing and Urban Affairs of the United States Senate, Washington, D.C., February 14, 2002.
11. Financial Accounting Standards Board, *FASB Response to SEC Study on the Adoption of a Principles-Based Accounting System*, July 2004.
12. See note 3.
13. See note 11.
14. See note 7.
15. Rebecca Toppe Shortridge and Mark Myring, "Defining Principles-Based Accounting Standards," *CPA Journal*, Vol. 74, No. 8, August 2004.
16. See note 4.
17. "Waiting to Converge: Global Accounting Standards," *California CPA*, July 2007.
18. Stephen A. Zeff, "The Evolution of US GAAP: The Political Forces Behind Professional Standards (Part II)," *CPA Journal*, Vol. 75, No. 2, February 2005.

CHAPTER 6

Different Standards for Different Companies?

As explained in previous chapters, the standard-setting work of Convergence is being done primarily by the Financial Accounting Standards Board (FASB) and the International Accounting Standards Board (IASB). The two boards have consistently portrayed the focus of their joint work as being the development a single set of high-quality financial reporting standards to be used in all countries. So it may strike you as surprising—and ironic—that as the FASB and the IASB work to eliminate differences in financial reporting standards among different *countries*, both boards are investigating the possibility of introducing differences in standards for different kinds of *companies*.

The possibility that different reporting entities in the United States will use different sets of financial reporting standards was mentioned briefly in Chapter 2. Recall that publicly held U.S. companies are almost certainly going to be required to adopt the set of global financial reporting standards that the FASB and IASB are developing. However, as explained earlier, privately held U.S. companies face three possible future scenarios, and in two of the three scenarios, privately held companies would use a set of financial reporting standards different from the set that publicly held companies would use.

The purpose of this chapter is to provide you with a deeper understanding of how the *convergence* of financial reporting standards among countries may end up fostering the *divergence* of standards among reporting entities, especially between publicly held and privately held companies in the United States.

Background

Even though they constitute only a tiny fraction of all U.S. businesses, publicly held companies have a disproportionately large impact on the

U.S. economy as a whole and on the economic welfare of U.S. citizens individually. Due to that impact, high-quality financial reporting by publicly held companies is widely considered to be an important public-policy goal. The pursuit of that goal has caused the process by which U.S. generally accepted accounting principles (GAAP) are set to focus primarily on serving the interests of users of financial statements issued by publicly held companies. And that focus has resulted in the widespread perception that U.S. GAAP is "out of sync" with the needs and capabilities of preparers, auditors, and users of financial statements issued by privately held companies.

With respect to financial reporting standards, the notion that "one size does *not* fit all" originated many decades ago. Subsequently, there has been an ongoing debate over whether all reporting entities should or should not use the same set of standards. That debate over financial reporting standards has often highlighted how user expectations and entity capabilities differ depending on whether the reporting entity is publicly or privately held. Because publicly held companies are commonly presumed to be "big" entities and privately held companies are commonly presumed to be "little" entities, the debate has traditionally been known as the *Big GAAP–Little GAAP* debate. But, over time, the less presumptive adjective *differential* has come into use, such that the debate is now often referred to as being about *differential financial reporting standards*.

U.S. GAAP currently contains relatively few differential provisions.[1] Of course, the U.S. Securities and Exchange Commission (SEC) imposes certain statutory financial reporting requirements on the publicly held companies under its jurisdiction—requirements that do not apply to privately held companies. Still, the SEC effectively requires U.S. public companies to use U.S. GAAP as set by the FASB.[2] And, although privately held companies in the United States are generally free to adopt any financial reporting standards they choose, the vast majority of privately held companies that have significant external users of their financial statements follow U.S. GAAP as a practical matter. Thus, in the United States, *non*-differential financial reporting standards are the norm.

Outside of the United States, the practice of differential reporting has traditionally varied from country to country. While IFRS contain no inherent differential provisions based on public-versus-private holdings of equity, many countries have implemented differential regulations regarding which entities are required or permitted to use IFRS and which entities are required or permitted to use country-specific financial reporting standards. In fact, the practice of differential reporting has actually become more widespread in recent years as many countries have required publicly held companies, but not privately held ones, to adopt IFRS.

One key point to note is that there is virtually no differential guidance in either U.S. GAAP or IFRS based on *entity size*,[3] although the SEC and regulators in other countries have implemented certain size-specific regulatory differences. For example, the SEC categorizes filers as *nonaccelerated*, *accelerated*, or *large accelerated* on the basis of size, generally measured by the filer's public float.[4] The SEC has used that size-based categorization in setting differential filing deadlines and rule-adoption dates for each category of filers (smaller public companies are generally allowed more time than larger companies to file and to adopt new rules). But financial reporting standards *per se* currently do not differ for publicly held U.S. companies of different sizes.

Private Company Financial Reporting Committee

In June 2006, the FASB and the American Institute of Certified Public Accountants (AICPA) began what they described as a "historic collaborative effort"[5] to explore the development of different accounting standards for privately held U.S. companies. As part of that effort, the FASB and the AICPA proposed to sponsor and fund a joint committee to serve as an additional resource to the FASB to further ensure that the views of private-company constituents are incorporated into the FASB's standard-setting process. Shortly thereafter, the FASB and the AICPA formed the Private Company Financial Reporting Committee (PCFRC), which held its inaugural meeting in May 2007.

The main objective of the PCFRC is to serve as a resource to the FASB staff during the research phase of FASB projects. At its inaugural meeting, the PCFRC decided that it would deliver formal position papers, in the form of recommendations, to the FASB when the PCFRC believes differences in GAAP related to private companies are warranted. Additionally, the Committee formed a resource group to obtain more input from private company constituents. The PCFRC plans to increase the number of resource group members to 1,000 by the end of 2008.

To date, the PCFRC has encouraged the FASB to:

- Defer the effective date of FASB Interpretation (FIN) No. 48 for "non-public" enterprises.[6]
- Require disclosure of the date through which subsequent events have been considered in financial statements in lieu of relying on users to infer that date from the issue date of the financial statements, as there is no formal issue date for private company financial statements.
- Consider the effects of Convergence and the IASB's Private Entities project (described later).

The PCFRC's current agenda is focused on the following existing standards:

- FASB Interpretation No. 46R, *Consolidation of Variable Interest Entities*
- FASB Statement No. 123R, *Share-Based Payment*
- FASB Statement No. 142, *Goodwill and Other Intangible Assets*

Additionally, the PCFRC is currently monitoring and may provide recommendations on the following FASB projects:

- Financial statement presentation
- FASB Statement 157, *Fair Value*, and the effects on private companies of Level 3 fair value inputs
- Revenue recognition

IASB's Small and Medium-Sized Entities Project

In contrast to the FASB's conservative and relatively recent steps toward differential financial reporting standards, the IASB has been working on an aggressive differential standard-setting initiative for many years—its Small and Medium-Sized Entities (SMEs) project. In September 2003 the IASB convened a meeting of financial reporting standard setters from around the world, most of whom expressed support for the development of country-neutral financial reporting standards specifically for SMEs. In June of the following year, the IASB issued a Discussion Paper titled *Preliminary Views on Accounting Standards for Small and Medium-Sized Entities*.

After extensive deliberation of comments received in response to the Discussion Paper, the IASB published an exposure draft (ED) of its *International Financial Reporting Standard for Small and Medium-Sized Entities* (IFRS for SMEs) in February 2007. Despite its name, the proposed IFRS for SMEs actually contained no inherent size criteria for establishing its scope. Rather, the standard is intended for entities that publish general-purpose financial statements for external users but that do not have public accountability.[7] As such, the scope is relatively consistent with the public-versus-private-company divide that is widely recognized in the United States. In keeping with the substance of the standard, at its May 2008 meeting the IASB agreed to change the name of the standard to IFRS for Private Entities.

In contrast to the full set of IFRS, the proposed IFRS for Private Entities:

- Eliminates topics that are not generally relevant to private entities
- Provides fewer accounting policy options
- Simplifies methods of recognition and measurement

- Reduces the number of required disclosures
- Uses "plain English" language

Starting in June 2007, the IASB conducted field tests of the proposed standard. Companies taking part in the field test were asked to:

- Submit their most recent annual financial statements under their existing accounting framework
- Prepare financial statements in accordance with the proposed standard for the same financial year
- Respond to a series of questions designed to identify any specific problems the company encountered in applying the ED

As of November 30, 2007, 161 letters of comment were received on the ED, and 115 SMEs from 20 countries had participated in the field tests. In April 2008, the IASB's SMEs Working Group met in London to discuss issues raised in ED comment letters and in the field tests. Assuming timely resolution of the issues raised, the IASB will issue a final IFRS for Private Entities in the first quarter of 2009.

Differential Standards: Three Questions

Today, the debate over differential financial reporting standards boils down to three related questions:

1. Should financial reporting standards differ among different kinds of entities?
2. If different kinds of entities should use different standards, how should the standards differ?
3. If standards differ, which standards should be used by which kinds of entities?

The next section will explore those questions.

Should Standards Differ?

A major argument in favor of differential financial reporting standards is that they have the potential to reduce the complexity of financial reporting for many, if not most, reporting entities. Specifically, the option to use simpler standards would be advantageous to the many entities that experience no gross incremental benefit from more-complex standards. Another argument for differential reporting standards is really an argument against nondifferential standards: A "one size fits all" set of standards imposes disproportionately high costs on smaller entities, often to the point where the gross incremental costs exceed the gross incremental benefits of applying the standards. To the extent that these arguments are valid, nondifferential standards unnecessarily stifle the competitiveness of reporting entities.

The main arguments against differential reporting standards are that differential standards would:

- Diminish the comparability of financial statements across entities of different kinds
- Diminish the quality of financial reporting for entities that use "inferior" standards
- Introduce wasteful segregation into standard-setting and professional education processes
- Amplify, rather than diminish, the problem of standards overload among users, auditors, and preparers of financial statements

Given the pros and cons of differential standards, the answer to the question "Should standards differ?" is likely to depend on whom you ask. For example, small-company and private-company professionals who work as preparers generally favor differential financial reporting standards, while large-company and public-company preparers generally do not care one way or the other. Those differing attitudes reflect a belief that the introduction of differential standards would result in changes to standards for small and privately held companies while leaving standards for large and publicly held companies unchanged. However, some small-company and private-company preparers want to avoid the stigma they fear might be associated with a "lesser" set of financial reporting standards—a stigma that could manifest itself as a higher cost of capital for their companies. Additionally, many privately held companies aspire to "go public" eventually and do not want to have to adopt a different set of financial reporting standards as part of what is already a challenging transition under the best of circumstances.

The attitudes of "inside" users of financial statements (e.g., majority owners, managers) tend to parallel those of preparers. That is, inside users of small-company and private-company financial statements generally favor differential financial reporting standards, while inside users of large-company and public-company financial statements generally do not care about differential standards.

Auditors tend to oppose differential financial reporting standards. It would certainly be more challenging for auditors to master more than one set of standards, even if one of those sets is simpler than or derived from the other. And the attitudes of "outside" users of financial statements (e.g., creditors, public investors) tend to be the same as auditors' attitudes, that is, outside users generally oppose differential standards because those users do not want to have to master multiple sets of standards.

While the foregoing generalizations help illustrate the diverse attitudes toward differential financial reporting standards that are held by participants in the financial reporting supply chain, they bring us no closer to a definitive answer to the question "Should standards differ?" However, in 2004–2005, the AICPA's Private Company Financial Reporting Task Force attempted to answer that question through a rigorous, comprehensive research study. On the basis of that study, the Task Force concluded unanimously that "GAAP for private companies should be developed based on concepts and accounting that are appropriate for the distinctly different needs of constituents of . . . financial reporting."[8] As a result of the Task Force's findings and recommendations, the governing Council of the AICPA passed a resolution in May 2005 that instructed "AICPA management to work with the Financial Accounting Foundation and the Financial Accounting Standards Board to identify and implement a process to develop GAAP for privately held, for-profit entities, which would result in recognition, measurement, and disclosure differences, where appropriate, from current GAAP as applied by public companies."[9] The subsequent execution of that directive led to the AICPA and FASB jointly forming the PCFRC to provide recommendations to the FASB regarding standards for privately held enterprises, as described earlier in this chapter.

Despite the seeming definitiveness of the Private Company Financial Reporting Task Force's conclusions, it did not take long for dissenting opinions to be heard. In particular, the Professional and Regulatory Response Committee of the National Association of State Boards of Accountancy (NASBA) publicly expressed its opinions on differential financial reporting standards in January 2006.[10] Specifically, the Committee commented that "Establishing separate, stand alone, standards for privately held companies would not be in the best interests of the public or the capital markets. . . ."

Meanwhile, the SEC had formed an "Advisory Committee on Smaller Public Companies." In its April 2006 final report to the SEC,[11] the Committee rejected the possibility of allowing differential financial reporting standards for different sizes of publicly held companies, although it did not directly address differential standards for privately held companies, as such companies generally do not fall under the jurisdiction of the SEC.

Of course, the parties whose attitudes toward differential financial reporting standards are most relevant to Convergence are the FASB and the IASB. As noted earlier, the FASB has partnered with the AICPA in forming the PCFRC. And the IASB has for many years been confidently progressing toward the development of differential standards through its SMEs project. Ultimately, the crucial point to recognize is that both the FASB and IASB are currently operating under the assumption that differential financial reporting standards for different kinds of entities *are* worth pursuing, even as the boards aggressively work to converge standards among countries.

How Should Differential Standards Differ?

The potential areas of difference among financial reporting standards for different entities are almost limitless. However, the main differences would most likely focus on the following areas:

- Accounting provisions (e.g., recognition and measurement)
- Reporting provisions (e.g., presentation and disclosure)
- The availability of explicitly described accounting policy options (or the lack thereof)
- Scope exceptions and exemptions
- Time frames for the adoption of new standards

Regardless of what the specific differences may be, there is widespread agreement that to the extent standards differ, they should differ in ways that will ensure the cost-effectiveness of whatever standards a reporting entity chooses or is required to adopt. This is generally understood to mean that relative to standards for other kinds of entities, differential standards for some entities would:

- Provide fewer explicitly described treatment options
- Require or allow simpler recognition and measurement methods
- Require fewer disclosures
- Permit extended adoption time frames
- Change less frequently

Also, if differential financial reporting standards were to exist for different kinds of entities, then standard setters would have to address the additional question of "To what degree should different sets of standards be coupled with each other?" In other words, should the standards that apply to one kind of entity be linked to or derived from the standards that apply to other kinds of entities? As with the differences in standards themselves, the possibilities for the degree of coupling are almost limitless. And the debate over the optimal degree of coupling is far from resolved.

Which Standards Should Be Used by Which Entities?

Enterprises are extremely diverse in ownership, size, composition, goals, strategy, operations, economics, risk exposure, and performance, as well as in their capacity to perform financial reporting effectively and efficiently. So what should be the basis for determining which differential standards should be used by which kinds of entities? As explained earlier in this chapter, the distinction that is generally perceived to be most relevant to differential financial reporting is the distinction between publicly and privately held entities.

Out of a total of approximately six million businesses in the United States (according the U.S. Census Bureau's Statistics of U.S. Businesses), such a distinction would segregate less than 1 percent of U.S. businesses into the publicly held group, leaving all other businesses in the privately held group. The "public-versus-private" dividing line was clearly acknowledged by the FASB and AICPA when they established the PCFRC (which considers "private" companies to be those that fail to satisfy the definition of an "issuer" as found in federal securities regulations[12]).

In the United States, it is difficult to make a case for further distinctions within each group, for example, on the basis of entity size.[13] According to the standards of the U.S. Small Business Administration, many publicly held companies are considered "small," however, the SEC's Advisory Committee on Smaller Public Companies stated flatly: "We have determined that different accounting standards should not be created for smaller and larger public companies."[14] And because nearly all privately held businesses are considered "small," there simply is not much impetus for sized-based differential reporting in the United States. Canada's Accounting Standards Board (AcSB) has similarly rejected a size test for implementing differential standards among non–publicly accountable entities.[15] And, as noted earlier, the proposed IFRS for private entities isn't scoped on the basis of size as much as it is scoped on the basis of other factors.

Perhaps the distinction among privately held U.S. companies that might end up having relevance is the distinction between companies that have significant external users of financial statements versus those that do not. But rather than attracting their own set of differential financial reporting standards, entities that have no significant external users of financial statements (e.g., owner-managed enterprises that do not rely on formally established credit facilities) are likely to be scoped out of standard setters' efforts to define differential standards.

How Convergence Is Fostering Differential Standards

Recall from earlier chapters that U.S. GAAP as we know it is becoming optional and will eventually go away. With virtual certainty, GAAP will go away for publicly held U.S. companies as a result of the SEC's eventually requiring the companies under its jurisdiction to adopt the set of global financial reporting standards that the FASB and IASB are developing. For privately held companies, current GAAP could disappear in one of two ways, both as a result of Convergence:

1. Allowing publicly held U.S. companies to adopt current IFRS and/or requiring publicly held U.S. companies to adopt future converged financial reporting standards may precipitate a "revolution" by privately held U.S. companies. If incentives to orient the U.S. standard-setting process toward public-company financial reporting disappear, private-company constituents would have the opportunity to assume control of the process, with one possible outcome being a radical reorientation of U.S. GAAP exclusively toward private-company financial reporting.
2. The IASB's continued development of the IFRS for Private Entities may result in the ready availability and widespread adoption of country-neutral differential financial reporting standards, which may prove attractive to privately held U.S. companies.

Of course, there are reasons why each of the above scenarios might fail to materialize. For example, maintaining a standard-setting infrastructure solely for privately held U.S. companies will not be feasible unless an effective funding mechanism is created to support that infrastructure.[16] Also, the IFRS for Private Entities is still a work in progress and may face resistance to adoption if the issues raised in comments on the ED as well as in field tests are not resolved to constituents' satisfaction in a timely manner. Finally, privately held companies in the United States may simply find it more practical to adopt the same future converged financial reporting standards that publicly held companies will adopt. But, regardless of the eventual outcome, U.S. financial managers in all kinds of enterprises should be prepared for change.

Conclusion

One nonintuitive result of the global Convergence of financial reporting standards among countries is that differential standards for publicly and privately held U.S. companies are an increasingly likely possibility. For the accounting profession and the millions of privately held U.S. companies, this will be an issue of great significance in the coming years.

The ultimate outcome depends on whether privately held U.S. companies move toward or away from country-neutral financial reporting standards, and if toward them, whether country-neutral standards eventually become differential in nature. The IASB's progress toward finalizing the IFRS for Private Entities will certainly be a major influence in determining the future of financial reporting standards for privately held companies in the United States. The PCFRC, which recognizes the growing pressures on privately held companies to adopt either full IFRS or the IFRS for Private Entities, will no doubt play a critical leadership role in shaping that future as well. Also, several committees within professional associations currently monitor the implications of Convergence for small and/or privately held companies and advocate on behalf of such companies. For example, the Institute of Management Accountants has a Small Business Financial and Regulatory Affairs Committee, and Financial Executives International has both a Committee on Private Companies as well as a Committee on Small and Mid-Size Public Companies.

As Convergence continues to bring profound change to the U.S. financial reporting supply chain, financial managers in privately held U.S. companies are strongly advised to stay abreast of the activities of the IASB, PCFRC, and other organizations in the area of differential standards.

Notes

1. An example of one of the relatively few differential provisions in U.S. GAAP is the exemption from the requirement to disclose earnings per share (under Statement of Financial Reporting Standards No. 128, *Earnings per Share*) that is available to entities without publicly held common stock (or potential common stock).
2. See Regulation S-X (17 CFR Part 210). Note, however, that in some cases SEC regulations require additional disclosures beyond those that are required under U.S. GAAP.
3. A notable exception is found in Statement of Financial Reporting Standards No. 126, *Exemption from Certain Required Disclosures about Financial Instruments for Certain Nonpublic Entities*, which contains, among other criteria, a size test based on the dollar value of an entity's total assets in order for the exemptions that are the subject of the Statement to be available to the entity.
4. A securities issuer's *public float* is the "the aggregate market value of common equity securities held by non-affiliates of the issuer." [Regulation M (17 CFR 242.100)]. "In 2002, the Commission divided public companies into two categories, 'accelerated filers' and 'non-accelerated filers,' and in 2005 added a third category of 'large accelerated filers,' providing scaled securities regulation for these three tiers of reporting companies. {FN56: See Acceleration of Periodic Report Filing Dates and Disclosure Concerning Website Access to Report, SEC Release No. 33-8128 (Sept. 16, 2002) [67 FR 58480]} Non-accelerated filers are fundamentally public companies with a public float below $75 million, and large accelerated filers are public companies with a public float of $700 million or more. {FN57: 17 CFR 240.12b-2. . .}" [Securities and Exchange Commission Advisory Committee on Smaller Public Companies, *Final Report of the Advisory Committee on Smaller Public Companies to the U.S. Securities and Exchange Commission*, April 23, 2006]

5. American Institute of Certified Public Accountants, *Private Company Financial Reporting* [web page accessed May 12, 2008], available at www.aicpa.org/ Professional+Resources/Accounting+and+Auditing/Private+Company+Financial +Reporting.

6. On February 1, 2008, the FASB issued FASB Staff Position FIN 48-2, *Effective Date of FASB Interpretation No. 48 for Certain Nonpublic Enterprises*, which deferred the effective date of FIN No. 48 for certain nonpublic enterprises to fiscal years beginning after December 15, 2007. On November 3, 2008, the FASB issued proposed FASB Staff Position FIN 48-c, *Effective Date of FASB Interpretation No. 48 for Certain Nonpublic Enterprises*, which would defer the effective date of FIN No. 48 for certain nonpublic enterprises to fiscal years beginning after December 15, 2008.

7. International Accounting Standards Board, *Exposure Draft of a Proposed IFRS for Small and Medium-Sized Entities*, paragraph 1.1, February 2007.

    "An entity has public accountability if: (a) it files, or it is in the process of filing, its financial statements with a securities commission or other regulatory organisation for the purpose of issuing any class of instruments in a public market; or (b) it holds assets in a fiduciary capacity for a broad group of outsiders, such as a bank, insurance entity, securities broker/dealer, pension fund, mutual fund or investment banking entity." [*Ibid.*, paragraph 1.2.]

    During the April 2008 meeting of the IASB's SMEs Working Group, which the author observed in person, Working Group members expressed considerable diversity of opinion over whether the proposed IFRS for SMEs was appropriately scoped on the basis of an entity's public accountability (or lack thereof) or whether the IFRS for SMEs should be scoped on the basis of entity size.

8. American Institute of Certified Public Accountants, *Private Company Financial Reporting Task Force Report*, February 28, 2005.

9. American Institute of Certified Public Accountants, Minutes of Meeting, Spring Meeting of Council, May 22–24, 2005.

    Note that the Financial Accounting Foundation (FAF) is the FASB's parent organization. It is responsible for the oversight, administration and finances of the FASB and the FASB's sister organization, the Governmental Accounting Standards Board (GASB).

10. Professional and Regulatory Response Committee of the National Association of State Boards of Accountancy, Letter to the Financial Accounting Standards Board, January 24, 2006, available at www.nasba.org/862571B900737CED/ 8A9DAECFBCCD3B09862571B900755BBE/$file/FASBLetter.pdf.

11. Securities and Exchange Commission Advisory Committee on Smaller Public Companies, *Final Report of the Advisory Committee on Smaller Public Companies to the U.S. Securities and Exchange Commission*, April 23, 2006.

12. Private Company Financial Reporting Committee, letter to the FASB staff about the definition of a private company, February 1, 2008, available at www.pcfr.org/ recommendations.html.

13. Other countries have implemented entity-size tests for differential financial re- porting standards. For example, the United Kingdom's Financial Reporting Stan- dard for Smaller Entities (FRSSE) incorporates a size test based on an entity's annual revenue.

14. See note 11.
15. See Accounting Standards Board, *Invitation to Comment: Financial Reporting by Private Enterprises*, 2007.
16. Currently, the FASB is funded primarily by publicly held companies as provided for by the Sarbanes-Oxley Act of 2002 (SOX). Reverting to the pre-SOX practice of relying on private donations would raise the same independence issues that led to the funding provision in SOX. Relying on the sales of standards publications and related products and services (which is currently a secondary but clearly profitable line of business for the FASB) would provide economic incentive for a standard setter to proliferate standards in order to ensure its own survival. And any attempt to shift costs to other participants in the financial reporting supply chain would certainly lead to backlash.

CHAPTER 7

Financial Statements: A First Look

As explained in Chapter 1, the flow of information in the financial reporting supply chain begins with reporting entities that prepare and communicate financial information about themselves. When preparing financial information to be communicated to other parties in the financial reporting supply chain, reporting entities typically "package" that information into a set of *financial statements*. After preparing financial statements for a reporting period, a company may choose to (or be required to) hand them over to an external auditor, who is then expected to render an opinion on the reliability of the information in the statements. Whether audited or not, paper and/or electronic copies of the financial statements are ultimately distributed to investors, creditors, and other users of the information contained in the statements.

Both U.S. generally accepted accounting principles (GAAP) and International Financial Reporting Standards (IFRS) contain standards that govern the manner in which financial statements are to be prepared and presented. Those standards effectively define the contents and formats of the financial statements, and also prescribe the accounting that must take place prior to the actual preparation of the statements. Of course, such standards currently differ between U.S. GAAP and IFRS. Therefore, depending on whether a reporting entity uses U.S. GAAP or IFRS, the contents of financial statements may differ quantitatively and qualitatively, and the formats of the statements may differ as well.

Because the process of Convergence will eventually eliminate differences in financial reporting standards among countries, financial statements in the future will differ far less from country to country than they do today. But Convergence will also cause future financial statements to be profoundly different from today's statements. To help you understand the impact that Convergence has had and will have on financial accounting and reporting in the United States, this chapter along with the remaining chapters in Part

Two will describe:

- The effects of recent standard-level Convergence initiatives on U.S. GAAP and IFRS
- Current similarities and differences between U.S. GAAP and IFRS at the standard level
- Specific ways in which both sets of standards will change as a result of continued Convergence between U.S. GAAP and IFRS

In particular, this chapter establishes a foundation for subsequent chapters by briefly comparing and contrasting financial statements prepared in accordance with current U.S. GAAP to financial statements prepared in accordance with current IFRS. Chapters 8 through 12 will examine, in detail, many specific aspects of recognition, measurement, presentation, and disclosure. Then Chapter 13, which concludes this part, will return to the financial statements and describe what they will look like under converged standards.

Along the way, many specific standards in both U.S. GAAP and IFRS will be cited. To ensure that references to specific standards will be understandable and useful to you, the following section will explain how standards will be referred to throughout the remainder of this book.

References to Standards

Both U.S. GAAP and IFRS are composed of several different types of guidance on financial accounting and reporting. In this book, the term *standards* refers broadly to all of the types of guidance found in U.S. GAAP and IFRS. In both sets of standards, a specific standard is usually referenced by citing the original pronouncement that established the standard (although as explained in the next subsection, such citations will soon become obsolete in U.S. GAAP due to the imminent introduction of the Financial Accounting Standards Board's [FASB's] *Accounting Standards Codification*).

This book does not cover all authoritative pronouncements nor is it intended to substitute for the pronouncements themselves. Furthermore, because authoritative guidance on financial accounting and reporting changes frequently, the information contained herein may quickly become out of date.

Standards in U.S. GAAP

Hereafter in this book, different types of pronouncements in U.S. GAAP will be cited using the following abbreviated references:

Reference	Type of Pronouncement
ARB	Accounting Research Bulletin
APB Opinion	Accounting Principles Board Opinion
SFAS	Statement of Financial Accounting Standards
FIN	FASB Interpretation
FSP	FASB Staff Position

While there are several additional types of pronouncements that are part of U.S. GAAP, they are not as authoritative as the types shown in the preceding list, and they are much less frequently cited in practice. This book does not contain references to those less authoritative pronouncements.

In July 2009, a major reorganization of U.S. GAAP is scheduled to take effect. At that time, the FASB's *Accounting Standards Codification* will completely change the way that U.S. GAAP is documented, updated, referenced, and accessed.[1] The change will impact the day-to-day work of nearly every financial professional who practices, teaches, or researches financial accounting and reporting in accordance with U.S. GAAP.

The Codification consists of:

- Topically organized content that will become the single authoritative source of U.S. GAAP, superseding all existing literature
- An online research system that will be the primary means of accessing the content

The Codification has not made substantive changes to standards, but it has effectively disassembled each existing authoritative pronouncement and reassembled the pieces into a new multilevel structure. Approximately 90 topics have been defined at the highest level in the structure. Within each topic, the levels continue with subtopics, then sections, then paragraphs. The paragraph level is actually the only level that contains substantive content; all higher levels in the structure exist merely to organize the paragraph-level content.

A numeric identifier is assigned to specific content at each level in the structure. Citing particular content in the Codification simply involves specifying the unique numeric "path" to the content through the topic, subtopic, section, and paragraph levels. The organizational structure and citation scheme are summarized in Exhibit 7.1.

Note that this approach organizes the Codification content without regard to the original standard setter or pronouncement from which the content was derived. Once the Codification is officially adopted by the FASB, references to standards will consist solely of the numeric identifiers used

EXHIBIT 7.1   Organizational Structure of FASB Accounting Standards
Codification

Level	Example Title	Example Citation
Topic	Inventory	330
Subtopic	Overall	330-10
Section	Initial Measurement	330-10-30
Paragraph	Cost Basis	330-10-30-1

in the Codification's organizational structure. To accommodate the forthcoming change, this book provides supplemental Codification references in
addition to the traditional, pronouncement-based references.

Standards in IFRS

In contrast to the multitude of individual pronouncements of many different types that make up U.S. GAAP, IFRS consist of only a few dozen
individual pronouncements of relatively few types. Unfortunately, the way
the pronouncements have been named by the International Accounting
Standards Board (IASB) and its predecessor, the International Accounting
Standards Committee (IASC), can cause confusion when referencing the
pronouncements.

Prior to the reorganization of the IASC into the IASB in 2001, the IASC
issued a series of primary pronouncements called "International Accounting
Standards." Subsequently, the IASB issued the same kind of pronouncements but called them "International Financial Reporting Standards." At the
time of the reorganization, the IASB chose to leave the older International
Accounting Standards in force without renaming them. The key point is
that today the term *International Financial Reporting Standards* is used
to refer collectively to both the newer standards promulgated by the IASB
(i.e., those that are specifically named "International Financial Reporting
Standards") and the older standards promulgated by the IASC (i.e., those
that are named "International Accounting Standards" and that still remain
in force). Although you may hear some people use the term *International
Accounting Standards* to refer collectively to both the older and newer
standards, that is not considered proper usage.

The potential confusion regarding references to pronouncements issued by the IASC and IASB extends to abbreviations of the pronouncements' names. For example, the abbreviation *IFRS* officially refers to an
individual pronouncement of the IASB, while *IFRSs* is the official abbreviation that refers collectively to multiple pronouncements of the IASB and/or
IASC. However, as noted in Chapter 1, the first abbreviation—*IFRS*—does
"double duty" in the United States. Depending on its context, that one

abbreviation may refer to an individual pronouncement or may refer collectively to multiple pronouncements.

The IASB has an associated interpretive body called the International Financial Reporting Interpretations Committee (IFRIC). The IASC had a similar interpretive body called the Standing Interpretations Committee (SIC). Both the IFRIC and SIC have issued pronouncements interpreting the standards promulgated by the IASB and IASC, respectively. The interpretative bodies of the IASB and IASC have functioned much like the FASB's Emerging Issues Task Force (EITF) in the United States, although IFRIC/SIC pronouncements are considered to be more authoritative within IFRS than similar EITF pronouncements are within U.S. GAAP. Use of the terms *International Financial Reporting Standards*, *IFRSs*, or *IFRS* (as a collective reference) are generally considered to refer to both the primary standard-setting pronouncements issued by the IASB/IASC as well as interpretative pronouncements issued by the IFRIC/SIC.

Hereafter in this book, different types of pronouncements will be cited using the abbreviated references shown below:

Reference	Type of Pronouncement
IAS	International Accounting Standard
SIC	Interpretation of the Standing Interpretations Committee
IFRS	International Financial Reporting Standard
IFRIC	Interpretation of the International Financial Reporting Interpretations Committee

Principal Financial Statements

Under U.S. GAAP, there are four principal kinds of financial statements. IFRS also define four principal kinds of financial statements that are nearly identical in purpose to their U.S. GAAP counterparts. Neither set of standards requires that the statements be called by specific names in practice, and even within the standards there is some variation in what the statements are called. The following list shows the most common or preferred names in each set of standards for each of the four kinds of statements:

U.S. GAAP	IFRS[2]
Balance Sheet	Statement of Financial Position
Income Statement	Statement of Comprehensive Income
Statement of Shareholder Equity	Statement of Changes in Equity
Statement of Cash Flows	Statement of Cash Flows

Even though there are currently many broad similarities between U.S. GAAP and IFRS regarding the principal financial statements, there are also many differences between the two sets of standards in their specific recognition, measurement, presentation, and disclosure provisions. Consequently, the contents and formats of actual financial statements that are prepared in accordance with one set of standards can be significantly different from the contents and formats of statements prepared in accordance with the other set of standards, even when the underlying transactions and events are the same. For example, IFRS requires the presentation of comparative information for the preceding reporting period in addition to the current reporting period, while U.S. GAAP does not.

Additionally, both U.S. GAAP and IFRS currently give financial statement preparers fairly wide discretion in certain areas such as the classification of items on the statements, the sequencing of items, the degree to which items are aggregated or not, and the extent to which totals and subtotals appear in the statements. Although the flexibility that preparers have under each current set of standards may be limited by government regulations in various jurisdictions (e.g., Regulation S-X of the U.S. Securities and Exchange Commission), the flexibility of existing standards can and does result in even greater variations among actual financial statements than can be explained by differences between the standards of U.S. GAAP and IFRS.

In every case, under both U.S. GAAP and IFRS, explanatory notes to the financial statements are considered an essential and integral part of the statements.

Balance Sheet

Under both U.S. GAAP and IFRS, the balance sheet is intended to show a "snapshot" of the entity's financial position. It presents the reporting entity's assets, liabilities, and owners' equity as of a specific point in time. Currently, the main overall differences between U.S. GAAP and IFRS with regard to the balance sheet are as follows:

- IFRS are more prescriptive than U.S. GAAP in terms of the specific line items, headings, and subtotals that must be presented.
- IFRS generally require the presentation of a classified balance sheet, with separate sections for current and noncurrent assets as well as current and noncurrent liabilities. U.S. GAAP does not require the presentation of a current/noncurrent classified balance sheet, but it is allowable under U.S. GAAP and very common in practice.
- The criteria for classifying assets and liabilities as current versus noncurrent differ slightly between U.S. GAAP and IFRS.

- It is nearly universal practice under U.S. GAAP to present assets and liabilities in order of decreasing liquidity (i.e., "cash first"). Under IFRS, presentation in order of increasing liquidity (i.e., "cash last") and decreasing liquidity are both common in practice.

Additional details about specific balance sheet items are discussed in Chapters 8 through 10.

Income Statement

Both U.S. GAAP and IFRS require the presentation of comprehensive income and its major components either on a single income statement or on two separate but closely related statements.[3]

Currently, the main overall differences between U.S. GAAP and IFRS with regard to the income statement are:

- IFRS are more prescriptive than U.S. GAAP in terms of the specific line items, headings, and subtotals that must be presented.
- Under IFRS, an entity must present expenses in a classified manner, with the "classification based on either the nature of the expenses or their function within the entity, whichever provides information that is reliable and more relevant."[4] Examples of "nature" classifications include depreciation, freight costs, and employee benefits. If using functional classifications, the entity must disclose its cost of sales expense explicitly and separately from other expenses. U.S. GAAP has no classification requirement for the income statement, but common practice under U.S. GAAP is to classify expenses on a functional basis.
- U.S. GAAP generally requires the separate presentation of any item that is both infrequent *and* unusual, along with certain other items, as "extraordinary." IFRS prohibit the presentation of any items as "extraordinary."

Additional details about specific income statement items are discussed in Chapter 11.

Statement of Shareholder Equity

Under both U.S. GAAP and IFRS, the statement of shareholder equity is intended to summarize how and why the balances of various equity accounts changed during the reporting period. The changes presented in the statement of shareholder equity reflect both the effects of comprehensive income and the effects of transactions with equity holders acting in their capacity as equity holders.

There are no substantive differences between U.S. GAAP and IFRS with regard to the statement of shareholder equity.[5] However, both sets of standards are minimally prescriptive, which has resulted in wide variations in presentation under both U.S. GAAP and IFRS.

Statement of Cash Flows

Detailed standards for the statement of cash flows exist in both U.S. GAAP and IFRS. Specifically, SFAS No. 95, *Statement of Cash Flows*, sets out the relevant standards under U.S. GAAP (alternatively, see FASB Codification Subtopic 230-10), while IAS 7, *Cash Flow Statements*, does so in IFRS.

Few substantive differences currently exist between U.S. GAAP and IFRS regarding the statement of cash flows. The differences that do exist relate mainly to the required or allowed classifications of interest and dividend transactions. However, differences in presentation can arise in practice because both U.S. GAAP and IFRS allow reporting entities to use either the direct method or the indirect method of reporting cash flows from operating activities.[6]

Additional details about the statement of cash flows are discussed in Chapter 11.

Conclusion

Now that you have an understanding of the overall similarities and differences in financial statements prepared under current U.S. GAAP and IFRS, you can learn more about the impact that Convergence will have on various specific aspects of financial accounting and reporting in Chapters 8 through 12. But still keep the "big picture" in mind: the FASB's and IASB's joint Convergence project on financial statement presentation will result in a complete overhaul of the contents and formats of the principal financial statements as we know them today. The profound impact of that project is discussed in Chapter 13, the concluding chapter of Part II.

Notes

1. For a comprehensive overview of the Codification, see Bruce Pounder, "Framing the Future: A First Look at FASB's GAAP Codification," *Journal of Accountancy*, May 2008. The Codification material in this section is adapted from that article.
2. The names of the financial statements under IFRS reflect changes made in the September 2007 revision of IAS 1, *Presentation of Financial Statements*.

3. The requirement to present comprehensive income was introduced into IFRS by the September 2007 revision of IAS 1, *Presentation of Financial Statements*. The revision effectively aligns IAS 1 with SFAS No. 130, *Reporting Comprehensive Income*, in U.S. GAAP (alternatively, see FASB Codification Subtopic 220-10). The revision to IAS 1 is effective for fiscal years beginning on or after January 1, 2009, with early adoption allowed.

4. IAS 1, *Presentation of Financial Statements* (as amended in August 2005), paragraph 88.

5. Differences between U.S. GAAP and IFRS regarding the statement of changes in equity (as it is known in IFRS) were effectively eliminated as a result of the September 2007 revision of IAS 1, *Presentation of Financial Statements*. The revision is effective for fiscal years beginning on or after January 1, 2009, with early adoption allowed.

6. It is interesting to note that use of the indirect method is far more common in practice, even though both U.S. GAAP and IFRS encourage entities to use the direct method.

CHAPTER 8

Fair Value and Related Measurement Issues

One of the central questions that financial reporting standards address is "How should a reporting entity's recognized assets and liabilities be measured?" Answering that question is not simply a matter of specifying which units of measurement (i.e., currency units) the reporting entity should use. More fundamentally, financial reporting standards must specify an approach (or approaches) to quantifying the economic worth of each asset and the economic burden of each liability.

There has been a long-running debate among participants in the financial reporting supply chain over various approaches to measuring the items that are recognized in financial statements. In recent years, one particular issue has become the focal point of that debate: whether *fair value* is an appropriate basis (or part of an appropriate basis) for measuring assets and liabilities. Within the context of the present controversy surrounding fair value, this chapter explores how Convergence will shape the measurement provisions of future financial reporting standards.

Background on Measurement

Guidance on measurement pervades both U.S. generally accepted accounting principles (GAAP) and International Financial Reporting Standards (IFRS). Currently, each set of standards incorporates multiple approaches to measuring assets and liabilities, with the approaches differing between the two sets of standards. The Financial Accounting Standards Board (FASB) and International Accounting Standards Board (IASB) view the diversity of measurement approaches that exists within and between U.S. GAAP and IFRS as representing a wealth of opportunities to improve and converge the measurement provisions of their respective standards. This section will provide background information to help you understand the major measurement-related issues that the FASB and IASB are attempting to address through their Convergence efforts.

Measurement Attributes

A *measurement attribute* is a quantitative characteristic that can be observed, calculated, or estimated for items in the financial statements. Familiar measurement attributes include *historical cost*, *replacement cost*, and *salvage value*. Of course, several different measurement attributes may be associated with a given item. For example, a specific asset may have a historical cost, a replacement cost, and a salvage value, along with other measurement attributes. That puts the onus on standard setters to prescribe which measurement attributes should be used for which items under which circumstances.

Traditionally, the FASB, IASB, and their predecessors have incorporated dozens of different measurement attributes into the measurement provisions of U.S. GAAP and IFRS. For that reason, each set of standards is often described as being based on a *mixed-attribute* measurement model. Over time, however, the FASB and IASB have become keenly aware of challenges that mixed-attribute measurement models impose on participants in the financial reporting supply chain. Measuring different balance sheet items in different ways leads to operational complexity for preparers and auditors, as does measuring the same balance sheet items in different ways under different circumstances. Mixed-attribute models have also been criticized by users of financial statements for unnecessarily impairing the comparability and other decision-useful characteristics of reported information.

Due to the recognized shortcomings of mixed-attribute measurement models, the FASB and IASB have been working on reducing the number of measurement attributes that are used in measuring assets and liabilities under U.S. GAAP and IFRS. The boards' efforts reflect a shared desire to converge on a smaller number of carefully chosen measurement attributes in future financial reporting standards.

Selection of Measurement Attributes

Ideally, a standard setter's choice of which measurement attributes to incorporate into a set of financial reporting standards is guided by the conceptual framework underlying the set of standards. As noted in Chapter 4, a conceptual framework will typically identify the overall objectives of financial reporting. It will also identify necessary and desirable qualitative characteristics of financial information (e.g., relevance, verifiability) along with key constraints (e.g., costs not to exceed benefits).

The FASB and IASB recognize that the use of different measurement attributes can lead to different degrees of consistency with the objectives, qualitative characteristics, and constraints described in the conceptual frameworks of U.S. GAAP and IFRS. In Phase C of the joint FASB-IASB conceptual framework project (see Chapter 4), the boards are attempting to select the set of measurement attributes that is most consistent with the objectives and qualitative characteristics that the boards are specifying in Phase A of the project. So far in Phase C, the boards have identified two key properties of measurement attributes that they consider highly relevant to the selection of the "best" measurement attributes for financial reporting purposes.

The first key property relates to the nature of a measurement attribute. In this regard, the boards have distinguished between two major kinds of measurement attributes: those that are *values* versus those that are *prices*. A value is "an entity-specific assessment of economic worth," whereas a price is "a value that is objectified through the operation of the marketplace."[1] The distinction between values and prices has significant implications for measurement:

- Measured values tend to be subjective in nature and are likely to be based on calculations and estimates rather than objective observations. For example, the expected cash flows associated with a financial instrument or other contractual arrangement could be used as the basis for establishing a balance sheet item's value. Expectations of cash flows from a given arrangement may vary from entity to entity, and the same stream of expected cash flows may have different values to different entities if an entity-specific discount rate is used to discount the future cash flows to their present value.
- Measured prices are based on actual or hypothetical market transactions from the perspective of the reporting entity. There are two fundamental kinds of prices: *entry prices* and *exit prices*. An entry price is the price that an entity pays to purchase an asset or receives to assume a liability from another entity. An exit price is the price that an entity receives to sell an asset or pays to have a third-party entity assume a liability. In the case of actual transactions, prices are observable, objective measurements. However, in the case of hypothetical transactions, prices may exhibit less objectivity. Depending on the liquidity and level of activity in the relevant market, it may not be possible to make an objective observation of price for a hypothetical transaction, and therefore it may be necessary to rely on calculations or estimates, which may or may not be based on objective inputs.

In addition to the value-price distinction, the second key property of measurement attributes is time orientation, that is, a "past, present, or future" characterization of the transaction, event, or state to which a measurement attribute refers. Given the two key properties, it is possible to define a relatively small set of basic measurement attributes that exhibit various possible combinations of the properties. That set includes, for example, *past entry price* and *future settlement value*.

Several of the basic measurement attributes (and slight variations thereof) are currently used in practice, although they may go by different names (e.g., *past entry price* is more commonly known as *historical cost*). More significantly, one particular basic attribute has captured the attention of both the FASB and IASB. It is the boards' focus on that attribute that lies at the heart of the current controversy over measurement standards.

Focus on Current Exit Price

Traditionally, past entry price (i.e., historical cost) has been the primary measurement attribute used to establish the carrying values of assets and liabilities under both U.S. GAAP and IFRS. But over time, the FASB, and to a lesser extent the IASB, have come to embrace *current exit price* as the preferred measurement attribute for assets and liabilities.

The primary rationale for the shift in emphasis from past entry price to current exit price is that the use of current exit price as a measurement attribute imbues reported financial information with greater relevance—a necessary qualitative characteristic—than past entry price or any other measurement attribute would. In particular, the FASB believes that past entry prices are often poorly reflective of the present economic significance of many assets and liabilities that increasingly appear on the balance sheet, such as derivative financial instruments. Additionally, most users of financial statements agree that current exit price makes a reporting entity's risk exposure and realized risks more transparent than past entry price does.

Not surprisingly, the FASB has taken steps to increase the overall use, as well as the consistency of implementation, of current exit price as a measurement attribute within U.S. GAAP. Both the FASB and IASB have also given serious consideration to current exit price as the potential cornerstone of measurement in future converged standards. But the boards' actions and intentions with regard to current exit price have provoked significant opposition from participants throughout the financial reporting supply chain. To understand the controversy that has arisen over measurement standards, it is necessary to understand the relationship between current exit price and fair value.

Current Exit Price and Fair Value

It is often asserted or implied that *fair value* is synonymous with *current exit price*. For example, Statement of Financial Accounting Standards (SFAS)

No. 157, *Fair Value Measurements*, states that "Fair value is the price that would be received to sell an asset or paid to transfer a liability in an orderly transaction between market participants in the principal or most advantageous market as of the measurement date." However, the actual relationship between fair value and current exit price under U.S. GAAP is more complicated. Additionally, the relationship is different under IFRS than it is under U.S. GAAP. Nevertheless, examining the controversy over current exit price as a measurement attribute is a good starting point for understanding the broader controversy over fair value.

Much of the opposition to fair value measurement is based on the assertion that current exit price is not an appropriate measurement attribute for many of the assets and liabilities to which the fair value measurement provisions of U.S. GAAP apply. Among participants in the financial reporting supply chain, opinions vary as to which balance sheet items should or should not be measured on the basis of current exit price. Various critics have argued that current exit price is *not* appropriate for:

- *Liabilities*, because liabilities are almost never extinguished by paying a third-party to assume them.
- *Nonfinancial assets*, because for most nonfinancial assets (with the exception of inventory) active, liquid markets do not exist.[2]
- *Held-to-maturity financial assets*, because the selling price of an asset that the entity does not intend to sell has little relevance.

An additional criticism of the fair value approach under Statement 157 is that it presumes a consensus of market participants about current exit price exists and is representationally faithful. However, a consensus is less likely to exist the less liquid, less tangible, and more risky a balance sheet item is.[3] Even when a consensus does exist, the market is not always "right" about economic worth, especially when the decision-influencing information that is known to market participants is inaccurate, incomplete, or untimely.

So while the FASB remains interested in the broad application of current exit price as a measurement attribute, critics continue to call for limiting its use. The dynamics of that conflict will certainly influence the measurement provisions of U.S. GAAP in the short term and globally converged standards in the long term.

Fair Value: Not One Measurement, But Many

Fair value under both U.S. GAAP and IFRS is often portrayed as a homogeneous measurement attribute, as if it were always measured the same way and always exhibited the same qualitative characteristics. But such portrayals are misleading. For example, the dominant fair value measurement approach under U.S. GAAP (i.e., the approach described in SFAS No. 157) involves a hierarchy of measurement methods that are applied to assets and liabilities, depending on what information is or is not available to the reporting entity.[4] As a result, the fair value of one balance sheet item may be determined in an entirely different way than the fair value of another balance sheet item, and the fair value of a particular balance sheet item may be determined in different ways under different circumstances. Furthermore, depending on the particular measurement method applied, fair value may effectively represent different measurement attributes and may exhibit significantly different qualitative characteristics.

The heterogeneity of fair value measurement in practice is an additional source of opposition to the use of fair value as a measurement basis. Fair value measurement differs somewhat between U.S. GAAP and IFRS, but a common criticism of financial statements prepared under both sets of standards is that fair values on an entity's balance sheet may lack sufficient objectivity, representational faithfulness, and/or verifiability when objective, observable information about current exit price is scarce, as it is in inactive or illiquid markets. An associated problem is that qualitative characteristics can and do vary significantly among the items on an entity's balance sheet and across entities as a result of diverse fair value measurement methods.

The FASB and IASB will continue to be challenged to demonstrate that the fair value measurement provisions of U.S. GAAP and IFRS are robust enough to provide decision-useful information under real-world circumstances.

Additional Opposition to Fair Value

Preparers and auditors have raised three practical criticisms of fair value measurement:

1. *Any measurement approach that requires periodic remeasurement involves more effort and cost than measurement approaches that require only initial measurement.* In most cases, the fair value standards of U.S. GAAP and IFRS require periodic "mark-to-market" accounting, which increases the burden on preparers and auditors, especially in contrast to historical cost accounting.
2. *The various measurement methods prescribed under the U.S. GAAP and IFRS fair value measurement hierarchies are often complex, costly, and time consuming to implement.* This is especially likely when objective, observable information is unavailable to the reporting entity. And again

this increases the burden on preparers, internal auditors, and external auditors. The risks to users of financial statements also increase as more measurements at the less objective levels of the fair value measurement hierarchies appear on the balance sheet, as such values are more susceptible to management manipulation.[5]

3. *Most preparers and auditors lack the full set of knowledge, skills, and abilities required to apply the fair value measurement hierarchies of U.S. GAAP and IFRS.* As valuation becomes increasingly critical to financial accounting and reporting under U.S. GAAP and IFRS, reporting entities find themselves relying more and more on external consultants and valuation experts. Many preparers have argued that something must be wrong with accounting standards when accounting can no longer be done by accountants.

Beyond the practical problems of implementing fair value measurement standards, two "big picture" criticisms have emerged as well:

1. *The inclusion in the income statement of changes in the fair values of balance sheet items may confuse users of financial statements.* This is especially true when unrealized gains/losses relate to assets held for use rather than for sale. Additionally, the inclusion of unrealized gains and losses due to changes in the fair values of assets and liabilities increases the volatility of the numbers in financial statements, which may obscure rather than illuminate relevant underlying phenomena.
2. *Existing fair value measurement standards may amplify cyclical swings in financial markets.* As the recent "credit crunch" has brought economic losses to various participants in the world's credit markets, stakeholders have looked for someone—or something—to blame, and many have found the scapegoat that they were looking for in fair value accounting.

Outlook for Improvement and Convergence

Given the multifaceted conflict that has arisen between standard setters and participants in the financial reporting supply chain over fair value measurement, we turn to examine how the conflict will likely be resolved going forward.

It appears that we may have reached a "high-water mark" for the use of current exit price as a measurement attribute. Based on the controversy that has arisen over the use of current exit price, neither it nor any one measurement attribute is likely to ever enjoy widespread acceptance as the "silver bullet" of measurement in financial reporting standards. In the future, other measurement attributes are likely to gain ground and become optional or required for at least some balance sheet items. Such alternative measurement attributes include past entry price (i.e., historical cost), current entry price (i.e., replacement cost), value-in-use, current settlement value, and future settlement value. Additionally, prescribed measurement attributes may become asymmetrical between assets and liabilities (e.g., financial assets might be measured at current exit price while financial liabilities might be measured at current settlement value). The overall result is likely to be the perpetuation of mixed-attribute measurement models, which may become even more "mixed" than they are now.

The heterogeneous hierarchy of fair value measurement is likely to persist; however, the umbrella term *fair value* may be dropped in favor of terminology that better distinguishes among the different measurement methods and attributes in the measurement hierarchy.

Criticisms of measuring balance sheet items at less objective levels in the current fair value measurement hierarchy are likely to be resolved by the issuance of additional guidance on measuring assets and liabilities when the relevant markets are inactive, illiquid, and/or inefficient. Still, accounting professionals will have little choice but to accept the necessity of learning contemporary valuation principles and techniques applicable to certain common circumstances.

The FASB and IASB have begun to address the issue of presenting in the income statement changes in the values of balance sheet items that result from periodic remeasurement (see Chapter 13 for more details on such presentation). Both boards are also likely to consider requiring more disclosures related to measurement attributes and methods.

A summary of recent developments in measurement standards and other guidance can be found in the appendix to this chapter.

Conclusion

Over time, the FASB and IASB have come to view assets and liabilities as the primary elements of financial reporting, and as a result, the boards have increased their interest in getting the measurement of assets and liabilities "right." But for the various reasons discussed in this chapter, the boards' attempts at improving the measurement of balance sheet items have not been widely embraced by participants in the financial reporting supply chain. The measurement provisions of U.S. GAAP and IFRS will undoubtedly be fine-tuned—and possibly even overhauled—as the FASB and IASB continue to improve and converge their standards.

Appendix: Summary of Recent Developments in Measurement Standards and Other Guidance

FASB

U.S. GAAP was significantly changed by the FASB's two most-recent pronouncements on fair value. In September 2006 the FASB issued SFAS No. 157, *Fair Value Measurements*, which was followed in February 2007 by SFAS No. 159, *The Fair Value Option for Financial Assets and Financial Liabilities*. SFAS No. 157 introduced a new standardized, hierarchical approach to measuring fair value but did not change which assets and liabilities are required or permitted to be measured at fair value. SFAS No. 159 expanded the set of items that entities are *permitted* to measure at fair value to include selected financial assets and liabilities without changing which items entities are *required* to measure at fair value.

The FASB appears to be aware that Statements 157 and 159 have challenged preparers and auditors in terms of the knowledge, skills, and abilities required to apply the fair value measurement provisions of U.S. GAAP. In January 2007 the FASB issued an invitation to comment (ITC) on "Valuation Guidance for Financial Reporting" to solicit comments from interested parties about the need, if any, for specific guidance related to the use of fair value measurements in financial reporting as well as the appropriate promulgating body and process. A public roundtable was subsequently held in April 2007 to foster discussion of the issues raised in the ITC. Then, in June 2007, the FASB announced the formation of a Valuation Resource Group to address issues relating to valuation for financial reporting. The resource group has since met on several occasions to discuss issues surrounding the implementation of the FASB's fair value standards.

Most recently, the FASB has considered issuing guidance to clarify the measurement of liabilities under SFAS No. 157.[6]

IASB

The IASB generally believes that fair value is the most relevant measurement basis for assets and liabilities. However, the IASB defines fair value differently from the FASB: fair value is "The amount for which an asset could be exchanged, or a liability settled, between knowledgeable, willing parties in an arm's length transaction."[7] With regard to assets, the IASB's definition revolves around *current price*, without specifically prescribing the use of entry or exit prices. With regard to liabilities, the IASB's definition calls for the use of *current settlement value*, which presumes that a liability will be settled with the current counterparty rather than transferred to a third party as under SFAS No. 157.

Through its Fair Value Measurement project, the IASB has been working to make the fair value measurement guidance in IFRS clearer, more internally consistent, and potentially more similar to U.S. GAAP. The project is not aimed at changing which assets and liabilities are required or permitted to be measured at fair value under IFRS.

The project's first consultative document was a discussion paper (DP) published in November 2006. That DP, whose comment period ended in May 2007, described the IASB's preliminary views of the provisions of the SFAS No. 157 and provided a comparison of SFAS No. 157 to existing fair value measurement guidance in IFRS. The DP also explored the possibility of replacing the definition of fair value and related measurement guidance in IFRS with a definition and guidance that reflects the IASB's preliminary views.

During 2008, notable progress was made on the Fair Value Measurement project in two areas:

1. A standard-by-standard review of the fair value provisions of IFRS was started and completed. The review will help the IASB determine whether fair value should be more clearly defined as current entry price, current exit price, or some other measurement attribute. The IASB will also consider whether to replace the use of the term *fair value* with one or more less ambiguous measurement attributes.
2. The IASB formed an Expert Advisory Panel to assist the board in reviewing best practices in the area of valuation techniques, and in formulating any necessary additional guidance on valuation methods for financial instruments and related disclosures when markets are no longer active.

Separately from its Fair Value Measurement project, the IASB issued a DP in March 2008 on "Reducing Complexity in Reporting Financial Instruments."[8] The DP identifies the use of a single measurement attribute for all financial instruments as an appropriate long-term step. It also identifies fair value as the only suitable single measurement attribute to use for all financial instruments. But recognizing the difficulties of implementing a general requirement to measure all financial instruments at fair value, the DP suggests alternative complexity-reducing approaches for the short-term.

The IASB plans to hold roundtable discussions in 2008 as part of its deliberation process for developing an exposure draft (ED) of an IFRS on fair value measurement guidance. The ED is scheduled for publication in mid-2009, with a final IFRS expected in 2010.

Other Resources

Several organizations have recently published ancillary guidance on fair value and related measurement issues. They include:

- **American Institute of Certified Public Accountants (AICPA):** Statement on Standards for Valuation Services (SSVS) No. 1, *Valuation of a Business, Business Ownership Interest, Security, or Intangible Asset* (June 2007)
- **International Valuation Standards Committee (IVSC):** *International Valuation Standards, 8th Edition* (August 2007)
- **Center for Audit Quality (CAQ):** White paper, *Measurements of Fair Value in Illiquid (or Less Liquid) Markets* (October 2007)
- **Public Company Accounting Oversight Board (PCAOB):** Staff Audit Practice Alert No. 2, *Matters Related to Auditing Fair Value Measurements of Financial Instruments and the Use of Specialists* (December 2007)

Additionally, the U.S. Securities and Exchange Commission (SEC) has conducted two roundtables to promote dialog about fair value and related measurement standards. The first roundtable, which examined fair value accounting standards in general, was held on July 9, 2008. The second roundtable, which examined the performance of IFRS and U.S. GAAP during the subprime crisis, was held on August 4, 2008.

*For the latest Convergence developments in fair value and other measurement guidance, visit **TheConvergenceGuidebook.com**.*

Notes

1. International Accounting Standards Board and Financial Accounting Standards Board, Attachment 3 to "Conceptual Framework—Measurement Roundtable Discussions" background materials, *Price/Value and Time Properties of Measurement Bases,* January 2007, available at www.iasb.org/Current+Projects/IASB+Projects/Conceptual+Framework/Round-table+discussions.htm.
2. The Financial Accounting Standards Board seems to be somewhat sympathetic to this argument; on February 12, 2008, FASB Staff Position No. FAS 157-2 was issued to delay the effective date of SFAS No. 157 for certain nonfinancial assets and nonfinancial liabilities.
3. See, for example, Warren D. Miller, "The Fatal Flaw in SFAS No. 157," *Strategic Finance,* August 2008.
4. "[F]air value ... is a combination of things and is not really one measurement basis at all." [FASB project manager Kevin McBeth, quoted in Ernst & Young,

"Update on the IASB/FASB Measurement Project," *Global EYe on IFRS*, August 2007].

5. For an excellent summary of those risks, see Chapter 1 of Alfred M. King, *Executive's Guide to Fair Value: Profiting from the New Valuation Rules*. Hoboken, NJ: John Wiley & Sons, 2008.

6. See Financial Accounting Standards Board, Proposed FSP FAS 157-c, *Measuring Liabilities under FASB Statement No. 157*, January 18, 2008.

7. International Accounting Standards Board, International Financial Reporting Standards Glossary of Terms, 2007.

8. On March 28, 2008, the Financial Accounting Standards Board issued an invitation to comment on the IASB's discussion paper, "Reducing Complexity in Reporting Financial Instruments."

CHAPTER 9

Major Asset Classes

This chapter summarizes the impact of Convergence on financial accounting and reporting for three major classes of assets:

1. Inventory
2. Property, plant, and equipment (PP&E)
3. Intangibles

Other specific financial statement items and issues will be addressed in subsequent chapters.

In these next several chapters that focus on specific financial statement items and issues, you will notice a common structure as each item or issue is addressed. First, a summary of major standards under both U.S. generally accepted accounting principles (GAAP) and International Financial Reporting Standards (IFRS) is presented, followed by a comparison the major provisions between U.S. GAAP and IFRS. In most cases, the comparison is followed by examples of how the standards have been applied in practice. Then, an outlook for how standards are likely to change in the future as a result of Convergence is provided. Finally, the broader implications of those likely changes to U.S. GAAP and IFRS are discussed.

Inventory

Summary of Major Standards

Exhibits 9.1 and 9.2 provide the major standards for inventory under U.S. GAAP and IFRS, respectively.

Comparison of Standards

Exhibit 9.3 shows a comparison of major provisions of standards for inventory between U.S. GAAP and IFRS.

EXHIBIT 9.1   Major Standards for Inventory under U.S. GAAP

Reference		Title	Last Revision
ARB	43	*Chapter 4: Inventory Pricing*	Jun 1953
SFAS	151	*Inventory Costs*	Nov 2004

See also FASB Codification Topic 330, *Inventory.*

EXHIBIT 9.2   Major Standards for Inventory under IFRS

Reference		Title	Last Revision
IAS	2	*Inventories*	Dec 2003
	41	*Agriculture*	Dec 2000

EXHIBIT 9.3   Comparison of Major Provisions of Standards for Inventory, U.S. GAAP versus IFRS

	U.S. GAAP	IFRS
Costing Method	Full absorption	Full absorption
Cost Flow Assumptions	Various methods permitted, including FIFO, LIFO, weighted average, specific identification, and retail method	Various methods permitted, including FIFO, weighted average, specific identification, and retail method. LIFO is prohibited.
Periodic Measurement	Lower of historical cost or "market value" (i.e., replacement cost constrained to a minimum of net realizable value less normal profit margin and a maximum of net realizable value)	Lower of historical cost or net realizable value
Recovery in Subsequent Fiscal Periods of Prior Reductions in Carrying Value	Prohibited	Required

Note 1: FIFO = first in, first out
Note 2: LIFO = last in, last out
Note 3: Net realizable value is defined as estimated selling price less estimated costs to complete and sell.

Examples of How Standards Are Applied in Practice

The following excerpts from notes to actual financial statements illustrate how standards for inventory are commonly applied in practice under U.S. GAAP and IFRS:

> **U.S. GAAP:** *We value our inventories at the lower of cost or market as determined primarily by the retail method of accounting, using the last-in, first-out ("LIFO") method for substantially all our Wal-Mart Stores segment's merchandise. Sam's Club merchandise and merchandise in our distribution warehouses are valued based on weighted average cost using the LIFO method. Inventories for international operations are primarily valued by the retail method of accounting and are stated using the first-in, first-out ("FIFO") method.... Under the retail method, inventory is stated at cost, which is determined by applying a cost-to-retail ratio to each merchandise grouping's retail value. The FIFO cost to retail ratio is based on the initial margin of the fiscal year purchase activity. The cost-to-retail ratio for measuring any LIFO reserves is based on the initial margin of the fiscal year purchase activity less the impact of any markdowns.[1]*

> **IFRS:** *Inventories are stated at cost or net realizable value, whichever is lower. Cost consists of all costs of purchase, cost of conversion and other costs incurred in bringing the inventories to their present location and condition, net of vendor allowances attributable to inventories. For certain inventories, cost is measured using the retail method, whereby the sales value of the inventories is reduced by the appropriate percentage gross margin. The cost of inventories is determined using either the first-in, first-out ("FIFO") method or the weighted average cost method, depending on their nature or use. Net realizable value is the estimated selling price in the ordinary course of business, less the estimated marketing, distribution and selling expenses.[2]*

Outlook for Convergence

In the future, U.S. GAAP and global converged standards are virtually certain to prohibit the *last in, first out* (LIFO) cost-flow assumption for inventory, as IFRS prohibit it now. The use of LIFO during times of rising inventory costs, as have been common in the United States for many decades, is highly distortive to the balance sheet and income statement.[3] Additionally, the application of LIFO in practice is often complex. Consequently, the elimination of the LIFO option would be widely regarded as an improvement over current U.S. GAAP.

Another area of likely future change relative to current U.S. GAAP is the replacement of the complex "Lower of Cost or Market Value" rule for inventory with the simpler "Lower of Cost or Net Realizable Value" rule currently found in IFRS. That change is likely to be accompanied by the substitution of a requirement to recover prior write-downs in the carrying value of inventory (as IFRS currently call for) for the current prohibition against doing so in U.S. GAAP.

Future converged standards may contain a specific standard for agricultural inventories much as IFRS do now (IAS 41). U.S. GAAP currently contains no standard specifically for agricultural inventories.

Implications of Potential Changes

The U.S. Internal Revenue Code has for many decades allowed taxpaying companies to use the LIFO cost-flow assumption for income tax reporting purposes. Historically, many U.S. companies have chosen to use LIFO because it provides significant tax benefits during times of rising inventory costs. As higher-cost inventory is assumed to be sold before lower-cost inventory, the reported cost-of-goods-sold expense is higher, taxable income is lower, and therefore the entity's tax liability is lower. But U.S. tax laws require companies that use LIFO for tax purposes to use LIFO for financial accounting and reporting purposes,[4] which is permissible under U.S. GAAP. Therefore, any prohibition of LIFO for financial accounting and reporting purposes would preclude companies from using LIFO for tax purposes under current law. Additionally, a company that ceases to use LIFO for tax purposes would effectively be forced to recognize the taxable income that it had avoided recognizing in earlier periods. For some U.S. companies, the ensuing tax liability could be financially catastrophic.

In contrast, the use of a simple, consistent periodic measurement model (i.e., lower of cost or net realizable value) would be of broad benefit to all parties throughout the financial reporting supply chain.

Property, Plant, and Equipment

Summary of Major Standards

Exhibits 9.4 and 9.5 provide the major standards for property, plant, and equipment (PP&E) under U.S. GAAP and IFRS, respectively.

Comparison of Standards

Exhibit 9.6 shows a comparison of major provisions of standards for PP&E between U.S. GAAP and IFRS.

EXHIBIT 9.4   Major Standards for Property, Plant, and Equipment (PP&E) under U.S. GAAP

Reference		Title	Last Revision
SFAS	34	*Capitalization of Interest Cost*	Oct 1979
	144	*Accounting for the Impairment or Disposal of Long-Lived Assets*	Aug 2001

Note: U.S. GAAP lacks authoritative pronouncements on the recognition and measurement of PP&E.
See also FASB Codification Topic 360, *Property, Plant, and Equipment*

Examples of How Standards Are Applied in Practice

The following excerpts from notes to actual financial statements illustrate how standards for PP&E are commonly applied in practice under U.S. GAAP and IFRS:

U.S. GAAP: *Property, plant and equipment are carried at cost less accumulated depreciation. Depreciation of property, plant and equipment, which includes assets under capital leases, is provided on the straight-line method over estimated useful lives. . . . The costs of repairs and maintenance are expensed when incurred, while expenditures for refurbishments and improvements that significantly add to the productive capacity or extend the useful life of an asset are capitalized. When assets are retired or sold, the asset cost and related accumulated depreciation are eliminated with any remaining gain or loss reflected in net earnings.*[5]

IFRS: *Land and buildings held for own use are stated at fair value at the balance sheet date. Increases in the carrying amount arising on revaluation of land and buildings held for own use are credited to the revaluation reserve in shareholders' equity. Decreases that offset previous increases of the same asset are charged against the revaluation reserve directly in equity; all other decreases are charged to the profit and loss account. Increases that reverse a revaluation decrease on the same asset previously recognized in net profit are recognized in the profit and loss*

EXHIBIT 9.5   Major Standards for PP&E under IFRS

Reference		Title	Last Revision
IAS	16	*Property, Plant, and Equipment*	Dec 2003
	23	*Borrowing Costs*	Mar 2007
	36	*Impairment of Assets*	Mar 2004

EXHIBIT 9.6   Comparison of Major Provisions of Standards for PP&E, U.S. GAAP versus IFRS

	U.S. GAAP	IFRS
Initial Measurement	Historical cost	Historical cost
Periodic Measurement	Historical cost less accumulated depreciation and impairment	Historical cost less accumulated depreciation and impairment or fair value (less accumulated depreciation and impairment subsequent to the last revaluation)
Construction Costs	Capitalize (including interest)	In general, capitalize; interest may be expensed or capitalized prior to 2009, must be capitalized after 2008
Maintenance and Repair Costs	Expense	Expense
Improvement Costs	Capitalize	Capitalize
Impairment Recognition	When asset's carrying amount exceeds the undiscounted expected future cash flows from the asset	When asset's carrying amount exceeds its recoverable amount
Impairment Measurement	Carrying amount vs. fair value (if active market exists, otherwise, Carrying amount vs. value-in-use)	Carrying amount vs. recoverable amount
Recovery of Impairment Losses	Prohibited	Required

Note 1: Value-in-use is defined as the discounted present value of the expected future cash flows from the asset.
Note 2: Recoverable amount is defined as the higher of the asset's value-in-use or "fair value less costs to sell."

account. Depreciation is recognized based on the fair value and the estimated useful life (in general 20–50 years). Depreciation is calculated on a straight-line basis. On disposal the related revaluation reserve is transferred to retained earnings. . . . The fair values of land and buildings are based on regular appraisals by independent qualified valuers. Subsequent expenditure is included in the assets carrying amount when it is probable that future economic benefits associated with the item will flow to the Group and the cost of the item can be measured reliably.[6]

Outlook for Convergence

Capitalization of construction interest is certain to be required in any converging and/or converged standards of the future. An option or requirement to use a fair value periodic measurement model for PP&E, similar to the option that currently exists in IFRS, is a likely possibility for U.S. GAAP and global converged standards. And the use of a more meaningful, integrated model for the recognition and measurement of impairment to PP&E, such as is found in IFRS today, is likely as well.

Implications of Potential Changes

Any shift toward the expanded use of a fair value model for periodic measurement of PP&E would certainly involve more cost and effort, as well as a qualitatively different skill set, than are currently necessitated by U.S. GAAP. Of course, under such a model, changes in the fair value of PP&E assets would result in greater volatility in balance sheet values, and would also bring greater volatility to cost-of-sales expense (as different depreciation amounts based on a fluctuating depreciable base are assigned to inventory each year). These would in turn bring more volatility to net income and shareholders' equity, and may result in more frequent triggering of impairment recognition.

At the same time, any use of an integrated model for the recognition and measurement of impairment would reduce the cost and effort required to determine and/or measure impairment.

Intangibles

Summary of Major Standards

Exhibits 9.7 and 9.8 provide the major standards for intangibles under U.S. GAAP and IFRS, respectively.

Comparison of Standards

Exhibit 9.9 shows a comparison of major provisions of standards for intangibles between U.S. GAAP and IFRS.

Examples of How Standards Are Applied in Practice

CAPITALIZATION VERSUS EXPENSING OF DEVELOPMENT COSTS   The following excerpts from notes to actual financial statements illustrate how standards for intangibles are commonly applied in practice under U.S. GAAP and IFRS,

EXHIBIT 9.7   Major Standards for Intangibles under U.S. GAAP

Reference		Title	Last Revision
SFAS	2	*Accounting for Research and Development Costs*	Oct 1974
	68	*Research and Development Arrangements*	Oct 1982
	86	*Accounting for the Costs of Computer Software to Be Sold, Leased, or Otherwise Marketed*	Aug 1985
	141(R)	*Business Combinations*	Dec 2007
	142	*Goodwill and Other Intangible Assets*	Jun 2001
	144	*Accounting for the Impairment or Disposal of Long-Lived Assets*	Aug 2001

See also FASB Codification Topic 350, *Intangibles—Goodwill and Other.*

particularly with regard to capitalization versus expensing of development costs:

> ***Transition from U.S. GAAP to IFRS:*** *Under IFRSs development costs are capitalized if specified criteria are met, while they are expensed under U.S. GAAP except for software development costs. For internally generated software all directly attributable costs (direct costs and directly attributable overheads) have to be recorded in the intangible assets under IFRSs, whereas under U.S. GAAP only direct costs are capitalized.*[7]

> ***Reconciliation of IFRS to U.S. GAAP:*** *The Group capitalizes certain development costs when it is probable that a development project will generate future economic benefits and certain criteria, including commercial and technological feasibility, have been met.... Capitalization ceases and [amortization] begins when the product becomes available to customers.... Capitalized development costs, comprising direct labor and related overhead, are amortized on a systematic basis over their expected useful lives between two and five years.... Under US GAAP, software development costs are similarly capitalized after the product has reached a certain degree of technological feasibility. However, certain non-software related development costs capitalized under IFRS are not capitalizable under US GAAP and therefore are expensed as incurred.*[8]

EXHIBIT 9.8   Major Standards for Intangibles under IFRS

Reference		Title	Last Revision
IAS	36	*Impairment of Assets*	Mar 2004
	38	*Intangible Assets*	Mar 2004
IFRS	3	*Business Combinations*	Jan 2008

EXHIBIT 9.9 Comparison of Major Provisions of Standards for Intangibles, U.S. GAAP versus IFRS

	U.S. GAAP	IFRS
Costs of Externally Acquired Intangibles	Capitalize	Capitalize
Costs of Internally Generated Intangibles	In general, expense as incurred; only "direct" costs are capitalized	Expense as incurred
Research Costs	Expense as incurred	Expense as incurred
Development Costs	Expense as incurred (except for certain computer software development)	Expense as incurred unless certain capitalization criteria are met
Other Business Start-up (Preoperating) Costs	Expense as incurred	Expense as incurred
Periodic Measurement of Intangible Assets	Historical cost less any accumulated amortization and impairment	In general, historical cost less any accumulated amortization and impairment; revaluation to fair value permitted only if the intangible asset trades in an active market (carrying value is reduced by accumulated amortization and impairment subsequent to the last revaluation)
Intangible Assets Considered to Have Limited Useful Lives	Amortize over useful life	Amortize over useful life
Intangible Assets Considered to Have Indefinite Useful Lives	Not amortized	Not amortized
Goodwill	Considered to have indefinite useful life	Considered to have indefinite useful life
Impairment Recognition	**If Limited Useful Life:** when asset's carrying amount exceeds the undiscounted expected future cash flows from the asset	When asset's carrying amount exceeds its recoverable amount

(Continued)

EXHIBIT 9.9 *(Continued)*

	U.S. GAAP	IFRS
	If Indefinite Useful Life: when asset's carrying amount exceeds its fair value (implied fair value in the case of Goodwill)	
Impairment Measurement	Carrying amount vs. fair value (if active market exists, otherwise, carrying amount vs. value-in-use)	Carrying amount vs. recoverable amount
Recovery of Impairment Losses	Prohibited	Required

Note 1: Value-in-use is defined as the discounted present value of the expected future cash flows from the asset.
Note 2: Recoverable amount is defined as the higher of the asset's value-in-use or "fair value less costs to sell."

IMPAIRMENT OF DEVELOPMENT COSTS   The following excerpt from notes to actual financial statements illustrates how standards for intangibles are commonly applied in practice under U.S. GAAP and IFRS, particularly with regard to impairment of development costs:

> ***Reconciliation of IFRS to U.S. GAAP:*** *Under IFRS, whenever there is an indication that capitalized development costs may be impaired the recoverable amount of the asset is estimated. An asset is impaired when the carrying amount of the asset exceeds its recoverable amount. Recoverable amount is defined as the higher of an asset's net selling price and value in use. Value in use is the present value of estimated discounted future cash flows expected to arise from the continuing use of an asset and from its disposal at the end of its useful life. . . . Unamortized capitalized development costs determined to be in excess of their recoverable amounts are expensed immediately. . . . Under US GAAP, the unamortized capitalized costs of a software product are compared at each balance sheet date to the net realizable value of that product with any excess written off. Net realizable value is defined as the estimated future gross revenues from that product reduced by the estimated future costs of completing and disposing of that product, including the costs of performing maintenance and customer support required to satisfy the enterprise's responsibility set forth at the time of sale. . . . For IFRS, discounted estimated cash flows are used to identify the existence of an impairment while for US GAAP undiscounted future cash flows are used. Consequently, an impairment could be required under IFRS but not under US GAAP.*[9]

PERIODIC MEASUREMENT The following excerpts from notes to actual financial statements illustrate how standards for intangibles are commonly applied in practice under IFRS, particularly with regard to periodic measurement.

> ***Transition from French GAAP to IFRS (Intangible Asset Revaluation):*** *Vivendi Universal has chosen not to apply the option provided for in IFRS 1, involving the remeasurement, as of January 1, 2004, of certain intangible and tangible assets at their fair value at that date.*[10]

> ***IFRS:*** *Intangible assets are stated at historical cost and are amortised on a straight-line basis over expected useful lives which usually vary from 3 to 10 years....*[11]

COMPREHENSIVE EXAMPLE OF HOW STANDARDS ARE APPLIED IN PRACTICE The following excerpt from notes to actual financial statements illustrates how standards for intangibles are commonly applied in practice under U.S. GAAP and IFRS:

SEC Form 20-F filed by Nokia Corporation on March 12, 2007

(Millions of Euros)

For the Years Ended December 31	2006	2005	2004
Profit attributable to equity holders of the parent reported under IFRS	4,306	3,616	3,192
US GAAP adjustments:			
Pensions	(1)	(3)	—
Development costs	(55)	10	42
Share-based compensation expense	(8)	(39)	39
Cash flow hedges	—	(12)	31
Amortization of identifiable intangible assets acquired	—	—	(11)
Impairment of identifiable intangible assets acquired	—	—	(47)
Amortization of goodwill	—	—	106
Other differences	22	(1)	(6)
Deferred tax effect of US GAAP adjustments	11	11	(3)
Net income under US GAAP	4,275	3,582	3,343

*"The US GAAP development cost adjustment reflects the reversal of cap-
italized non-software related development costs under US GAAP net of
the reversal of associated amortization expense and impairments under
IFRS. The adjustment also reflects differences in impairment methodolo-
gies under IFRS and US GAAP for the determination of the recoverable
amount and net realizable value of software related development costs."*

Outlook for Convergence

It is possible that future U.S. GAAP and global converged standards, like
current IFRS, will require the capitalization of certain development costs,
with software development costs not being a special case as in U.S. GAAP
today. And similar to the situation with PP&E, the use of a more meaningful, integrated model for the recognition and measurement of impairment
to intangible assets, such as is found in IFRS today, is likely. Also, a single,
consistent impairment model for different types of assets (e.g., PP&E and intangibles) would be an improvement over U.S. GAAP's multiple impairment
models.

Implications of Potential Changes

A shift toward required capitalization of development costs would be expected to have a short-term positive impact on the net income of companies
that invest heavily in development. Such a shift may also lead to less volatility in income if development costs fluctuate widely from year to year.

Again, as with PP&E, any use of an integrated model for the recognition
and measurement of impairment would reduce the cost and effort required
to determine and/or measure impairment while improving the quality of
financial reporting.

Conclusion

This chapter has summarized the impact of Convergence on financial accounting and reporting for inventory, PP&E, and intangibles. While Convergence can be expected to improve the quality of financial reporting
with regard to those items, reporting entities that use U.S. GAAP today will
certainly face significant technical and managerial challenges as a result
of Convergence. And as you will see in the next few chapters, the upside-
downside nature of the impact of Convergence is not unique to the financial
statement items addressed in this chapter.

Notes

1. SEC Form 10-K filed by Wal-Mart Stores, Inc., on March 27, 2007.
2. SEC Form 20-F filed by Royal Ahold on March 29, 2007.
3. See Paul B. W. Miller and Paul R. Bahnson, "Fortress LIFO Is Crumbling: It's About Time," *WebCPA*, January 28, 2008.
4. This is known as the "conformity requirement" of Section 472 of the U.S. Internal Revenue Code.
5. SEC Form 10-K/A filed by Starbucks Corporation on December 21, 2006.
6. SEC Form 20-F filed by ING Groep N.V. on April 20, 2007.
7. Intershop Communications AG 2005 Annual Report.
8. SEC Form 20-F filed by Nokia Corporation on March 12, 2007.
9. Ibid.
10. SEC Form 20-F filed by Vivendi Universal on June 29, 2005.
11. SEC Form 20-F filed by Stora Enso Oyj on March 29, 2007.

CHAPTER 10

Other Balance Sheet Items

This chapter summarizes the impact of Convergence on financial accounting and reporting for the following balance-sheet items:

- Leases
- Pensions and other postretirement benefit obligations
- Deferred income tax effects

Leases

Summary of Major Standards

Exhibits 10.1 and 10.2 provide the major standards for leases under U.S. generally accepted accounting principles (GAAP) and International Financial Reporting Standards (IFRS), respectively.

Comparison of Standards

Exhibit 10.3 shows a comparison of major provisions of standards for leases between U.S. GAAP and IFRS.

Outlook for Convergence

While lease accounting standards under U.S. GAAP and IFRS are substantially converged in principle, they differ at the most detailed level of guidance. But more significantly for Convergence, lease standards under both U.S. GAAP and IFRS are widely viewed as failures at promoting *substance-over-form* accounting in practice, a situation that neither the Financial Accounting Standards Board (FASB) nor the International Accounting Standards Board (IASB) consider acceptable.

EXHIBIT 10.1   Major Standards for Leases under U.S. GAAP

Reference		Title	Last Revision
SFAS	13	*Accounting for Leases*	Nov 1976
	23	*Inception of the Lease*	Aug 1978
	28	*Accounting for Sales with Leasebacks*	May 1979
	91	*Accounting for Nonrefundable Fees and Costs Associated with Originating or Acquiring Loans and Initial Direct Costs of Leases*	Dec 1986
	98	*Accounting for Leases: Sale-Leaseback Transactions Involving Real Estate, Sales-Type Leases of Real Estate, Definition of the Lease Term, and Initial Direct Costs of Direct Financing Leases*	May 1988
FIN	19	*Lessee Guarantee of the Residual Value of Leased Property*	Oct 1977
	21	*Accounting for Leases in a Business Combination*	Apr 1978
	23	*Leases of Certain Property Owned by a Governmental Unit or Authority*	Aug 1978
	24	*Leases Involving Only Part of a Building*	Sep 1978
	26	*Accounting for Purchase of a Leased Asset by the Lessee during the Term of the Lease*	Sep 1978
	27	*Accounting for a Loss on a Sublease*	Nov 1978
FSP	FAS 13-2	*Accounting for a Change or Projected Change in the Timing of Cash Flows Relating to Income Taxes Generated by a Leveraged Lease Transaction*	July 2006

See also FASB Codification Topic 840, *Leases*.

EXHIBIT 10.2   Major Standards for Leases under IFRS

Reference		Title	Last Revision
IAS	17	*Leases*	Dec 2003
SIC	15	*Operating Leases—Incentives*	Jul 1999
	27	*Evaluating the Substance of Transactions in the Legal Form of a Lease*	Dec 2001
IFRIC	4	*Determining Whether an Arrangement Contains a Lease*	Dec 2004

EXHIBIT 10.3 Comparison of Major Provisions of Standards for Leases, U.S. GAAP versus IFRS

	U.S. GAAP	IFRS
Capital Leases (Finance Leases)	Leases that transfer substantially all the benefits and risks of ownership from the lessor to the lessee	Leases that transfer substantially all the benefits and risks of ownership from the lessor to the lessee
Operating Leases	Any lease that is not a capital lease	Any lease that is not a capital lease
Subclassification of Capital Leases into Sales-Type Leases and Direct Financing Leases	Yes	No
Lessor's Discount Rate for Computing Present Value of Minimum Lease Payments	Lease's implicit rate	Lease's implicit rate
Lessee's Discount Rate for Computing Present Value of Minimum Lease Payments	Lessee's incremental borrowing rate, unless the lease's implicit rate is known and is lower	Lease's implicit rate if practicable; otherwise, lessee's incremental borrowing rate
Gain/Loss on Sale-Leaseback Transaction—Capital Lease	Generally, recognize over lease term; recognize over the remaining useful life of the asset if certain criteria are met	Recognize over lease term
Gain/Loss on Sale-Leaseback Transaction—Operating Lease	Recognize over lease term	Immediately recognize (some exceptions exist)

Note: For sale-leaseback transactions under U.S. GAAP, the seller must recognize a loss immediately to the extent that the presale carrying value of the property exceeds the property's fair value.

Both boards believe that financial accounting and reporting standards should emphasize substance over form. In other words, transactions and events that have similar underlying economics should be accounted for similarly, regardless of any nominal or legal distinctions. The desire of the FASB and the IASB to overcome the form-over-substance nature of current lease accounting will dominate their Convergence efforts going forward. Additionally, the boards will attempt to address valid criticisms of the recognition and measurement provisions of current lease standards as being overly reliant on arbitrary, bright-line rules.

Through their joint long-term project on leases, the FASB and the IASB are working to implement a *right-of-use* model (also known as a *rights-and-obligations* model) in their respective standards as well as in future converged standards. Such a model will eliminate the distinction between operating and capital leases, with the result that *every* lease will be represented on the lessee's balance sheet by a combination of an asset and a liability, similar to the way capital leases are accounted for today.

In conjunction with the introduction of a single right-of-use model for all leases, Convergence on a method for measuring lease-related assets and liabilities is inevitable. Not surprisingly, the boards have given strong consideration to fair value in their measurement deliberations to date. Additionally, the FASB and IASB can be expected to establish a single method for seller-lessees to recognize gains/losses on sale-leaseback transactions.

In mid-2008, the FASB and IASB decided to limit the short-term scope of their joint leasing project in order to be able to develop an improved, converged standard in a shortened time frame. As a result of that decision, the immediate focus of the project is on developing improvements to lease accounting by lessees; lessor accounting will not be addressed until much later in the future. The boards expect to issue an enhanced lease-accounting standard in 2011.

Implications of Potential Changes

Any lessees that currently classify leases as operating leases will face radically different accounting for those leases in the future. For example, implementation of a single, pervasive, right-of-use model for lease accounting will provide lessors and lessees with far fewer opportunities to structure lease transactions around the bright-line rules of current standards in a manner that enables lessees to keep lease-related assets and liabilities off of their balance sheets. Thus, implementation of a right-of-use model will certainly result in the recognition of more assets and liabilities on lessees' balance sheets than is the case today under either U.S. GAAP or IFRS.

One impact of those changes is that lessees' financial leverage metrics, such as the liabilities-to-equity ratio, will be altered. Also, measures of lessees' financial performance will be affected significantly.[1] For example, earnings before interest, taxes, depreciation, and amortization (EBITDA, a widely used, non-GAAP profit measure on which many loan covenants and executive compensation plans are based) will increase for lessees that currently recognize rent expense from operating leases. Under a right-of-use model, instead of rent expense, lessees would recognize interest expense, amortization expense, and expenses for executory costs, with interest and amortization not being deducted in arriving at EBITDA as rent expense is. However, to the extent that interest, amortization, and executory-cost expenses in total exceed the present rent expense, the lessee's net income will decrease. The reduction in net income, coupled with an increase in lease-related assets on lessees' balance sheets, means that lessees are likely to exhibit a significantly lower return on assets (ROA).

Additionally, a reclassification of the cash outflows for rent payments into a combination of executory costs paid, interest paid, and a reduction of lease-related liabilities will cause operating cash flow to increase—and financing cash flow to decrease—by the amount deemed to represent a reduction of liabilities.

Of course, a strict asset-and-liability approach to accounting for all leases will involve greater cost and effort for reporting entities and their auditors. But benefits of improved lease accounting—arising from greater comparability, consistency, and transparency—will clearly accrue to users of financial statements.

Pensions and Other Postretirement Benefit Obligations

Summary of Major Standards

Exhibits 10.4 and 10.5 show the major standards for pensions and other postretirement benefit obligations under U.S. GAAP and IFRS, respectively.

EXHIBIT 10.4 Major Standards for Pensions and Other Postretirement Benefit Obligations under U.S. GAAP

Reference		Title	Last Revision
SFAS	87	*Employers' Accounting for Pensions*	Dec 1985
	88	*Employers' Accounting for Settlements and Curtailments of Defined Benefit Pension Plans and for Termination Benefits*	Dec 1985
	106	*Employers' Accounting for Postretirement Benefits Other Than Pensions*	Dec 1990
	132(R)	*Employers' Disclosures about Pensions and Other Postretirement Benefits*	Dec 2003
	158	*Employers' Accounting for Defined Benefit Pension and Other Postretirement Plans*	Sep 2006

See also FASB Codification Topics 715, *Compensation—Retirement Benefits*, and 712, *Compensation—Nonretirement Postemployment Benefits*.

EXHIBIT 10.5   Major Standards for Pensions and Other Postretirement Benefit
Obligations under IFRS

Reference		Title	Last Revision
IAS	19	*Employee Benefits*	Dec 2004
IFRIC	14	*The Limit on a Defined Benefit Asset, Minimum Funding Requirements and their Interaction*	Jul 2007

Comparison of Standards

Exhibit 10.6 provides a comparison of the major provisions of standards for pensions and other postretirement benefit obligations under U.S. GAAP and IFRS.

Examples of How Standards Are Applied in Practice

The issuance of Statement of Financial Accounting Standards (SFAS) No. 158 brought U.S. GAAP and IFRS largely into convergence with regard to reflecting on the balance sheet the funded status of pensions and other postretirement benefit obligations, although somewhat different language is used in each set of standards. Exhibits 10.7 and 10.8 provide excerpts from notes to actual financial statements illustrate the effects of SFAS No. 158 adoption under U.S. GAAP. Note how the year-to-year change in stockholders' equity attributable to SFAS No. 158 adoption (via an increase in pretax accumulated other comprehensive loss) differs dramatically between Exhibits 10.7 and 10.8, to the point of creating a deficit balance in the latter exhibit.

Outlook for Convergence

Both the FASB and IASB are committed to the long-term improvement and Convergence of financial reporting standards for pensions and other postretirement benefit obligations. However, the boards' work in this area has not been nearly as coordinated as it has been in other areas. Consequently, while U.S. GAAP and IFRS are each gradually improving, it is more accurate to describe the boards' short-term improvement efforts as "leapfrogging" each other rather than "converging."

In particular, the FASB has been working to enhance the plan-asset disclosures required under SFAS No. 132(R) while the IASB has been focused on other issues. In March 2008, the FASB published FASB Staff Position (FSP) No. 132(R)-a, which contains proposed changes to U.S. GAAP that are

EXHIBIT 10.6 Comparison of Major Provisions of Standards for Pensions and Other Postretirement Benefit Obligations, U.S. GAAP versus IFRS

	U.S. GAAP	IFRS
Sponsor's Recognition of Assets/Liabilities for Defined Benefit Plans	The difference between the fair value of plan assets and the plan's benefit obligation	The plan's benefit obligation, adjusted for unrecognized actuarial gains and losses and unrecognized prior service cost, reduced by the fair value of plan assets, and if the result is an asset, limited to the net total of unrecognized actuarial losses and prior service cost, plus the present value of available refunds and reductions in future contributions to the plan; in some circumstances, an additional liability must be recognized under the Minimum Funding Requirement provisions of IFRIC 14
Periodic Measurement of Benefit Obligation for Defined Benefit Plans	For a pension plan, the "Projected Benefit Obligation"; for any other postretirement benefit plan, the "Accumulated Postretirement Benefit Obligation"	"Projected Unit Credit Method"
Recognition of Unrecognized Prior Service Costs (UPSC—changes in the plan's obligations that result from changes to the plan when the effects of the plan changes on the plan's obligations are dependent on employee service rendered in prior periods)	Amortize over the expected average remaining service years of active participating employees; recognize changes in the unamortized portion of UPSC immediately in Other Comprehensive Income	Recognize immediately to the extent that the UPSC relates to former employees or to active employees already vested; otherwise, amortize over the average period until the amended benefits become vested

(Continued)

EXHIBIT 10.6 *(Continued)*

	U.S. GAAP	IFRS
Recognition of Actuarial Gains and Losses (the effects of differences between previous actuarial assumptions and actual experience; also the effects of changes in actuarial assumptions)	Using the "10% Corridor Test," amortize any "out of corridor" portion of accumulated unrecognized actuarial gains/losses over the expected average remaining service years of active participating employees; recognize changes in the unamortized portion of accumulated unrecognized actuarial gains/losses immediately in Other Comprehensive Income.	Using the "10% Corridor Test," amortize any "out of corridor" portion of accumulated unrecognized actuarial gains/losses over the expected average remaining service years of the participating employees; alternatively, immediate recognition of actuarial gains/losses in their entirety as Other Comprehensive Income is permitted
Periodic Measurement of Plan Assets	Fair value	Fair value (subject to the limits of IFRIC 14)

Note: Under the "10% Corridor Test," the absolute value of net accumulated gains and losses is compared to a "corridor" amount that is 10 percent of the greater of the defined benefit obligation or the fair value of plan assets. Different accounting treatment may be applied depending on whether gains/losses are "in corridor" (i.e., less than the corridor amount) or "out of corridor" (i.e., greater than the corridor amount).

EXHIBIT 10.7 SEC Form 20-F filed by Deutsche Bank on March 27, 2007 (Millions of Euros)

Pension-Related Items	Prior to SFAS 158 Adjustment	SFAS 158 Adjustment	Post SFAS 158 Adjustment
Prepaid assets	1,277	(754)	523
Accrued liabilities	(158)	(36)	(194)
Pretax accumulated other comprehensive loss (income)	7	790	797

For the 12 Months Ending Dec 31	2006	2005
Total liabilities	1,093,422	962,225
Total stockholders' equity	32,808	29,936
Total liabilities and stockholders' equity	1,126,230	992,161

intended to improve disclosures about plan assets. The proposed amendments include:

- A principle for disclosing the fair value of categories of plan assets based on the types of assets held in the plan
- Categories of plan assets that, if significant, should be disclosed

EXHIBIT 10.8 Ford Motor Company 2006 Annual Report (Millions of U.S. Dollars)

Pension-Related Items	Prior to SFAS 158 Adjustment	SFAS 158 Adjustment	Post SFAS 158 Adjustment
Prepaid assets	4,112	(2,542)	1,570
Intangible assets	1,466	(1,466)	—
Accrued liabilities	(30,276)	(5,355)	(35,631)
Pretax accumulated other comprehensive loss (income)	4,534	9,363	13,897

For the 12 Months Ending Dec 31	2006	2005
Total liabilities	280,860	254,895
Minority interests	1,159	1,122
Total stockholders' equity	(3,465)	13,442
Total liabilities and stockholders' equity	278,554	269,459

- Disclosures about the nature and amount of concentrations of risk arising within or across categories of plan assets
- Disclosures about fair value measurements similar to those required by SFAS No. 157, *Fair Value Measurements*

Also in March 2008, the IASB issued a discussion paper (DP) on its preliminary views regarding amendments to International Accounting Standard (IAS) 19. The main areas for improvement explored in the IASB's DP relate to accounting for:

- Gains and losses on defined-benefit plan assets
- Benefit obligations that are based on a promised return on contributions where the promised return is linked to an asset or to an index

Implications of Potential Changes

While the enhanced disclosures proposed in FSP No. 132(R)-a would provide better information to users of financial statements, they would clearly increase the burden on preparers and auditors. Going forward, the FASB plans to investigate recognition, measurement, and disclosure issues related to multiemployer postretirement benefit plans. The board will also consider presentation issues for all plans within the context of the joint financial statement presentation project (see Chapter 13 for detailed information about that project).

The IASB's DP proposes the removal of options for deferring the recognition of gains and losses on the assets of defined-benefit plans. Such deferrals misleadingly smooth volatility in the income statement, and are considered to significantly distort both the income statement and balance sheet. The fundamental issue raised in the DP is not whether gains and losses on plan assets should be recognized fully and immediately—the IASB clearly believes that they should—but rather *how* those gains and losses should be measured and presented in the income statement in order to be most decision useful.

In its DP, the IASB has also proposed a more accurate way of classifying a plan based on the nature of the plan's benefit promises. Specifically, for plans whose benefits are based on a promised return on contributions where the promised return is linked to an asset or to an index, the IASB has proposed an additional category of plan—*contribution based*—that would eliminate the ambiguity that exists under current standards for classifying such plans as either "defined benefit" or "defined contribution." Additionally, contribution-based benefit obligations would be measured and presented differently from obligations under either of the two existing categories.

Deferred Income Tax Effects

Summary of Major Standards

Exhibits 10.9 and 10.10 show the major standards for deferred income tax effects under U.S. GAAP and IFRS, respectively.

Comparison of Standards

Exhibit 10.11 provides a comparison of the major provisions of standards for deferred income tax effects of U.S. GAAP and IFRS.

Examples of How Standards Are Applied in Practice

The following excerpts from notes to actual financial statements illustrate how standards for deferred income tax effects are commonly applied in practice under U.S. GAAP and IFRS:

> ***German entity using U.S. GAAP:*** *In July 2006, the FASB issued FASB Interpretation No. 48, "Accounting for Uncertainty in Income Taxes" ("FIN 48"). FIN 48 prescribes a recognition threshold and measurement attribute for the financial statement recognition and measurement of a tax position taken or expected to be taken in a tax return. The Interpretation also provides guidance on derecognition, classification, interest (that we will classify in our financial statements as interest expense, consistent with our current accounting policy) and penalties, accounting in interim periods, disclosure, and transition. FIN 48 is effective in fiscal years beginning after December 15, 2006. The provisions of FIN 48 are to be applied to all tax positions upon initial adoption, with the cumulative effect adjustment reported as an adjustment to the opening balance of*

EXHIBIT 10.9 Major Standards for Deferred Income Tax Effects under U.S. GAAP

Reference		Title	Last Revision
SFAS	109	*Accounting for Income Taxes*	Feb 1992
FIN	48	*Accounting for Uncertainty in Income Taxes*	Jun 2006

See also FASB Codification Topic 740, *Income Taxes*.

EXHIBIT 10.10 Major Standards for Deferred Income Tax Effects under IFRS

Reference		Title	Last Revision
IAS	12	*Income Taxes*	Oct 2000

EXHIBIT 10.11   Comparison of Major Provisions of Standards for Deferred Income
Tax Effects, U.S. GAAP versus IFRS

	U.S. GAAP	IFRS
Tax Rate to Use in Measuring Deferred Tax Assets/Liabilities	Enacted	Enacted or "substantively enacted"
Recognition of Deferred Tax Assets	Recognize in full; use valuation allowance for any amount for which realization is doubtful	Recognize amount to the extent of "probable" realization
Recognition of Deferred Tax Liabilities	Recognize in full	Recognize in full
Classification of Deferred Tax Assets and Liabilities	Current or noncurrent, based on the classification of the underlying asset or liability	Noncurrent
Uncertain Tax Positions	Recognize only positions that are "more likely than not" to be sustained upon examination by the taxing authority	Based on management's expectations

*retained earnings. The cumulative effect of less than € 5 million will be
recognized as a decrease to beginning retained earnings on the adoption
of FIN 48 on January 1, 2007.*[2]

IFRS: *As reported [in 2005], GSK's largest unresolved tax issues were
with the US Internal Revenue Service (IRS) . . . in respect of transfer prices
related to the Glaxo heritage products. . . . On 11th September 2006, GSK
and the IRS agreed to a resolution of their dispute. Under the agreement, GSK has made gross payments to the IRS of approximately $3.3
billion. . . . The settlement resolved all the transfer pricing issues in dispute
for the period 1989–2000, which were due to go to trial in February 2007,
and also covers the subsequent years 2001–2005. GSK had previously
made provision for the dispute and this settlement did not have any significant impact on the Group's reported earnings or tax rate for the year.*[3]

Outlook for Convergence

For several years, the FASB and IASB have been working to converge financial reporting standards for deferred income tax effects. Although U.S. GAAP

and IFRS are based on similar principles, several specific differences exist between the two sets of standards. For example, U.S. GAAP contains certain exceptions to the principles on which it and IFRS are based, whereas IFRS contain different exceptions to the same principles. The most significant difference, however, is the detailed guidance regarding uncertain tax positions that exists in U.S. GAAP but not IFRS. That guidance is documented in the highly-controversial FASB Interpretation (FIN) 48, *Accounting for Uncertainty in Income Taxes*.

Until recently, the FASB had planned to make several minor modifications to U.S. GAAP while the IASB planned to make several major modifications to IFRS as interim steps toward developing a converged standard. However, in mid-2008, the FASB began to consider whether the IASB's forthcoming revised version of IAS 12 would sufficiently address the shortcomings in U.S. GAAP that the FASB was attempting to remedy with the minor modifications it had planned. The FASB's initial analysis of the situation led it to conclude that the forthcoming revised version of IAS 12 would indeed represent major progress toward an improved, converged standard with one glaring exception—it would not incorporate FIN 48–type guidance regarding uncertain tax positions. The IASB has expressed reluctance to incorporate such guidance into IFRS, especially given the high level of opposition to FIN 48 in the United States.

Implications of Potential Changes

One clear implication of the FASB and IASB's efforts to develop an improved, converged standard on accounting for income taxes is that the boards will carry forward the fundamental principles on which U.S. GAAP and IFRS are now based while eliminating existing exceptions to those principles. Otherwise, the future common standard is likely to retain most characteristics of current U.S. GAAP (e.g., the intraperiod tax allocation requirements of SFAS No. 109), with the "wild card" being whether and how the kind of guidance now found in FIN 48 is incorporated into that standard.

Conclusion

Although U.S. GAAP and IFRS are substantially converged today in the areas of leases and postretirement benefit obligations, neither the FASB nor the IASB is satisfied with today's standards. Those two areas serve as prime examples of how multilateral standard-level Convergence will produce common standards that are very different from today's standards.

In contrast, accounting for deferred income tax effects is an area that will be largely characterized by unilateral standard-level Convergence, with

IFRS being likely to change far more than U.S. GAAP will. The various sections of this chapter serve to remind us that Convergence is a complex phenomenon that is playing out in multiple ways simultaneously.

Notes

1. See Charles W. Mulford, *The Effects of Lease Capitalization on Various Financial Measures: An Analysis of the Retail Industry*, Georgia Tech Financial Analysis Lab, June 12, 2007; and Charles W. Mulford, *Lease Capitalization, Financial Agreements and EBITDA*, Georgia Tech Financial Analysis Lab, November 2007, both available at www.mgt.gatech.edu/finlab.
2. SEC Form 20-F filed by Deutsche Bank Corporation on March 27, 2007.
3. SEC Form 20-F filed by GlaxoSmithKline on March 2, 2007.

CHAPTER 11

Reporting Financial Performance

This chapter summarizes the impact of Convergence on the following areas of financial accounting and reporting, each of which relates to one or more key measures of financial performance:

- Revenue recognition and measurement
- Income statement
- Cash flow

Revenue Recognition and Measurement

Summary of Major Standards

Exhibits 11.1 and 11.2 show the major standards for revenue recognition and measurement under U.S. generally accepted accounting principles (GAAP) and International Financial Reporting Standards (IFRS), respectively.

Comparison of Standards

Exhibit 11.3 provides a comparison of major provisions of standards for revenue recognition and measurement between U.S. GAAP and IFRS.

Outlook for Convergence

As with many other standard-setting projects on the FASB's and IASB's agendas, the boards have been working together for many years to improve and converge financial reporting standards for revenue recognition and measurement. But, unlike most other joint projects, the boards have very little to show for their extensive efforts in this area.

The boards' lack of progress cannot be ignored, since improving revenue recognition and measurement standards has long been considered a top priority.[1] The existing revenue provisions of U.S. GAAP and IFRS

121

EXHIBIT 11.1   Major Standards for Revenue Recognition and Measurement under U.S. GAAP

Reference		Title	Last Revision
ARB	45	*Long-Term Construction-Type Contracts (as amended)*	Oct 1955
SFAS	48	*Revenue Recognition When Right of Return Exists*	Jun 1981

Note: U.S. GAAP lacks a comprehensive, authoritative pronouncement on the recognition and measurement of revenue.
See also FASB Codification Topic 605, Revenue Recognition

EXHIBIT 11.2   Major Standards for Revenue Recognition and Measurement under IFRS

Reference		Title	Last Revision
IAS	11	*Construction Contracts*	Dec 1993
	18	*Revenue*	Dec 1998
IFRIC	13	*Customer Loyalty Programmes*	Jun 2007

EXHIBIT 11.3   Comparison of Major Provisions of Standards for Revenue Recognition and Measurement, U.S. GAAP versus IFRS

	U.S. GAAP	IFRS
Has Comprehensive, Authoritative Pronouncement	No	Yes
Detailed Implementation Guidance Provided	Yes	No
Permitted Revenue Recognition Methods for Construction Contracts	■ Percentage of completion ■ Completed contract	■ Percentage of completion ■ Cost recovery
Specific Guidance Provided on Sales of Goods with Right of Return	Yes	No

continually confound preparers, auditors, and regulators, albeit for different reasons depending on which set of standards is involved. In fact, improper revenue recognition has consistently been identified as a leading cause of financial restatements among public U.S. companies.[2] Thus, the stakes are high and progress toward improving and converging revenue standards is imperative.

Currently, the revenue recognition and measurement standards of U.S. GAAP and IFRS are based on similar fundamental principles that determine whether and when revenue should be recognized. But while IFRS offer little guidance beyond the principles, U.S. GAAP contains an estimated 200-plus individual provisions that are widely scattered throughout dozens of different pronouncements. To make matters worse, those provisions are often inconsistent with the fundamental principles and with each other.

The fundamental principles that currently underlie both sets of standards are based on an *earning process* approach to revenue recognition. Under that approach, a necessary (but not sufficient) criterion for recognizing revenue is that the process of earning the revenue must be complete. Typically, completion of an earning process requires that certain events occur, that measurable progress is made toward a specific objective, or that an entity perform certain activities.

In working toward Convergence on improved revenue recognition standards, the FASB and IASB have abandoned the earning process approach and have instead embraced an *asset-liability* approach. Under the asset-liability approach, revenue is recognized by direct reference to changes in assets and liabilities of the entity, rather than by direct reference to critical events or activities as in the earning process approach.

Specifically, under the asset-liability approach to revenue recognition, an entity that exchanges promises with its customers (e.g., ABC Company promises to deliver a widget to XYZ Company in exchange for XYZ Company's promise to pay ABC Company $100) is viewed as acquiring specific rights or obligations depending on the particulars of the promises exchanged and the sequence in which the parties fulfill their respective promises. For example, if an entity does not receive payment from a customer yet fulfills its promise to deliver goods to that customer, the entity has a right (i.e., to receive payment from the customer) but no corresponding performance obligation. Conversely, if the entity receives payment from the customer prior to fulfilling its promise to deliver goods, the entity has a performance obligation (i.e., to deliver goods to the customer) but no corresponding right. The central concept of the asset-liability approach is that such rights should be recognized as assets of the entity while such obligations should be recognized as liabilities of the entity. Revenue is recognized under the asset-liability approach whenever such rights-based assets arise or whenever such performance-obligation liabilities are satisfied.

There are a few revenue-recognition issues that the FASB and IASB have yet to resolve, such as developing specific criteria for determining when a performance obligation exists and when it should be considered satisfied. The boards must also address accounting for conditional arrangements, for example, those in which the customer has the right to return delivered goods for a refund (or in lieu of paying for the goods). But the FASB and IASB remain committed to basing future revenue recognition standards on the asset-liability approach rather than on the present earning process approach.

In contrast to the relative ease and swiftness with which the FASB and IASB achieved consensus on the asset-liability approach to revenue recognition, the boards' debate over how revenue should be *measured* has dragged on for years. Under the asset-liability approach, how revenue is measured depends heavily on how the underlying rights-based assets and performance-obligation liabilities are measured as well as how changes to the carrying values of those assets and liabilities are measured.

To date, many specific revenue-measurement issues have been extensively deliberated by the FASB and IASB. For example, the boards have devoted substantial effort into identifying the appropriate attribute for the initial measurement of rights-based assets and performance-obligation liabilities arising from an entity's arrangements with its customers. From a practitioner's perspective, the "obvious" choice is the stipulated sales price of an arrangement. Recently, the boards have gravitated toward that measurement basis, which they refer to as "customer consideration," but neither board has been willing to assume that customer consideration is the only measurement basis worth exploring.

Beyond the fundamental debate over an appropriate initial-measurement attribute for assets and liabilities arising from revenue arrangements with customers, the FASB and IASB have debated many other measurement issues, including:

- Whether revenue-arrangement assets and liabilities should be periodically remeasured
- Whether the same initial measurement attribute and periodic remeasurement model should be used for both assets and liabilities
- Whether revenue should be recognized when the carrying values of revenue-arrangement assets and liabilities change as a result of periodic remeasurement
- How the measured amounts of assets, liabilities, and revenue should be allocated to individual deliverables in multiple-element arrangements

After recently reducing the short-term scope of their joint revenue project in the interest of developing an improved, converged standard in a shortened time frame, the FASB and IASB expect to issue their first discussion paper for public comment by the end of 2008.

Implications of Potential Changes

Convergence will result in an overhaul of the fundamental revenue-recognition and revenue-measurement principles in both U.S. GAAP and IFRS. On the basis of new principles, reporting entities can expect to see changes in whether, when, and to what extent they should recognize revenue.

Convergence will also eliminate the confusing thicket of rules-based revenue standards and other practices that we have today. Compared to present U.S. GAAP, converged standards on revenue recognition and measurement will be far less complex and will contain far fewer inconsistencies and exceptions (such as special treatment for software revenue). The FASB's Codification of U.S. GAAP will greatly facilitate the boards' progress in this area.

Income Statement

Summary of Major Standards

Exhibits 11.4 and 11.5 show the major standards for the income statement under U.S. GAAP and IFRS, respectively.

EXHIBIT 11.4   Major Standards for the Income Statement under U.S. GAAP

Reference		Title	Last Revision
APB Opinion	30	*Reporting the Results of Operations—Reporting the Effects of Disposal of a Segment of a Business, and Extraordinary, Unusual and Infrequently Occurring Events and Transactions*	Jun 1973
SFAS	128	*Earnings per Share*	Feb 1997
	129	*Disclosure of Information about Capital Structure*	Feb 1997
	130	*Reporting Comprehensive Income*	Jun 1997
	160	*Noncontrolling Interests in Consolidated Financial Statements*	Dec 2007

See also FASB Codification Topics:

- 205, *Presentation of Financial Statements*
- 220, *Comprehensive Income*
- 225, *Income Statement*
- 235, *Notes to Financial Statements*
- 260, *Earnings per Share*

EXHIBIT 11.5 Major Standards for the Income Statement under IFRS

Reference		Title	Last Revision
IAS	1	*Presentation of Financial Statements (fiscal years beginning before 2009)*	Aug 2005
		Presentation of Financial Statements (fiscal years beginning after 2008; early application permitted)	Sep 2007
	33	*Earnings per Share*	Dec 2003

Comparison of Standards

Exhibit 11.6 provides a comparison of major provisions of standards for the income statement under U.S. GAAP and IFRS.

Examples of How Standards Are Applied in Practice

The following excerpts from notes to actual financial statements illustrate how standards for the income statement are commonly applied in practice under U.S. GAAP and IFRS.

U.S. GAAP (pre-SFAS No. 160):

(Millions of U.S. Dollars)

For the Three Months Ended March 31	*2007*
Operating revenues	*22,584*
Total operating expenses	*18,788*
Operating income	*3,796*
Equity in earnings of unconsolidated businesses	*160*
Other income and (expense), net	*48*
Interest expense	*(485)*
Minority interest	*(1,154)*
Income before provision for income taxes, discontinued operations, and extraordinary item	*2,365*
Provision for income taxes	*(881)*
Income before discontinued operations and extraordinary item	*1,484*
Income from discontinued operations, net of tax	*142*
Extraordinary item, net of tax	*(131)*
Net income	*1,495*

EXHIBIT 11.6 Comparison of Major Provisions of Standards for the Income Statement, U.S. GAAP versus IFRS

	U.S. GAAP	IFRS
Ordinary Items vs.	Extraordinary items (infrequent **and** unusual)	Prohibit distinction based on "ordinariness" or lack thereof
Noncontrolling Interests in Investee Reported by Controlling Investor	**CURRENT:** Noncontrolling share in the income of subsidiaries is presented as an expense in the consolidated income statement **NEW*:** Noncontrolling share in the income of subsidiaries is separately stated in the consolidated income statement	Noncontrolling share in the income of subsidiaries is separately stated in the consolidated income statement
Earnings per Share Disclosures	**Required:** Basic (and diluted for entities with complex capital structures) ■ Income from continuing operations ■ Discontinued operations ■ Extraordinary items ■ Net Income	**Required:** Basic and diluted ■ Income from continuing operations ■ Discontinued operations ■ Net income (Disclosure of other per-share amounts is permitted)
Method to Compute the Dilutive Effects of Convertible Instruments	"If Converted" method	"If Converted" method
Method to Compute the Dilutive Effects of Options, Warrants, and Similar Exercisable Instruments	"Treasury Stock" method	"Treasury Stock" method

*For annual reporting periods beginning on or after December 15, 2008.

In January 2007, the Bolivarian Republic of Venezuela (the Republic) declared its intent to nationalize certain companies, including [Compañía Anónima Nacional Teléfonos de Venezuela (CANTV)]. On February 12, 2007, we entered into a Memorandum of Understanding (MOU) with the Republic. The MOU provides that the Republic will offer to purchase all of the equity securities of CANTV, including our 28.5% interest, through

public tender offers.... The Republic launched the public tender offers
on April 9, 2007.... Based upon the terms of the MOU and our current
investment balance in CANTV, we recorded an extraordinary loss on
our investment of $131 million, net of tax in the first quarter of 2007.[3]

IFRS[4]:

(Millions of Euros)

For the 12 Months Ending Dec 31	2006
Revenues	152,809
Cost of sales	(126,137)
Gross profit	26,672
Selling expenses	(11,519)
General administrative expenses	(5,989)
Research and noncapitalized development costs	(4,228)
Other operating income, net	777
Share of profit (loss) from companies accounted for using the equity method, net	(150)
Other financial income (expense), net	(74)
Earnings before interest and taxes (EBIT)	5,489
Interest expense, net	(401)
Profit before income taxes	5,088
Income tax expense	(1,305)
Net profit	3,783
Minority interest	(39)
Profit attributable to shareholders of DaimlerChrysler AG	3,744

Outlook for Convergence

The IASB has recently amended IFRS to require the presentation of comprehensive income in a manner similar to that required by current U.S. GAAP. However, more significant changes are in store for both U.S. GAAP and IFRS as a result of the joint FASB-IASB financial statement presentation project (see Chapter 13).

In recent years, users of financial statements prepared in accordance with U.S. GAAP have become concerned about abuses of management's discretion to classify some income statement items as "extraordinary." Those concerns are likely to lead to the elimination of such a classification from

U.S. GAAP. That would pave the way for further Convergence with IFRS, which currently prohibit the presentation of any income statement items as "extraordinary."

The FASB has recently changed how *noncontrolling interests* (formerly known as *minority interests*) are presented in consolidated income statements. That long-overdue change brings U.S. GAAP into alignment with current IFRS.

U.S. GAAP and IFRS are currently relatively converged on standards for computing earnings per share (EPS) as presented in the income statement. However, the FASB and IASB still have a project on their agendas left over from the early days of collaboration between the boards on developing an improved converged standard for EPS. In August 2008, the IASB issued an exposure draft (ED) on proposed changes to its EPS standard. Simultaneously with the issuance of the IASB's ED on EPS, the FASB issued its own ED of a proposed Statement of Financial Accounting Standards (SFAS) on EPS. The standards proposed in the EDs would eliminate the differences between IAS 33 and SFAS No. 128, with limited exceptions. The key issues in this project revolve around the kinds of instruments that should factor into the computation of the weighted number of shares outstanding, that is, the denominator of the basic and diluted EPS calculations.

Implications of Potential Changes

Convergence of U.S. GAAP and IFRS on income statement matters will leave fewer opportunities for the management of a reporting entity to manipulate income from continuing operations as a result of arbitrary classifications of certain items as extraordinary. And there will be new twists in computing basic and diluted EPS, with changes to the "Treasury Stock" and "If Converted" methods expected.

Cash Flow

Summary of Major Standards

Exhibits 11.7 and 11.8 show the major standards for cash flow under U.S. GAAP and IFRS, respectively.

EXHIBIT 11.7   Major Standards for Cash Flow under U.S. GAAP

Reference		Title	Last Revision
SFAS	95	*Statement of Cash Flows*	Nov 1987

See also FASB Codification Topics:

- 205, *Presentation of Financial Statements*
- 230, *Statement of Cash Flows*
- 235, *Notes to Financial Statements*

EXHIBIT 11.8   Major Standards for Cash Flow under IFRS

Reference		Title	Last Revision
IAS	7	*Cash Flow Statements*	Dec 1992

EXHIBIT 11.9   Comparison of Major Provisions of Standards for Cash Flow, U.S. GAAP versus IFRS

	U.S. GAAP	IFRS
Classification of Interest Paid	Operating	Either operating or financing
Classification of Interest Received	Operating	Either operating or investing
Classification of Dividends Paid	Financing	Either operating or financing
Classification of Dividends Received	Investing	Either operating or investing
Bank Overdrafts	Excluded	Included only if they form an integral part of the entity's cash management
Disclosure of Cash Flow per Share in Financial Statements	Prohibited	Permitted

Comparison of Standards

Exhibit 11.9 provides a comparison of the major provisions of standards for cash flow under U.S. GAAP and IFRS.

Examples of How Standards Are Applied in Practice

The following excerpts from notes to actual financial statements illustrate how standards for cash flow are commonly applied in practice under IFRS:

> **IFRS Example 1:** *Under the IFRS format, the amounts of taxation accrued and taxation paid are shown separately within "cash flow from operating activities," rather than within working capital movements. Reported "cash flow from operating activities" in 2004 has increased by $1.4 billion with an offset in cash flow from investing and financing activities. This is mainly due to: The different presentation of interest (interest paid is now included in financing activities and interest received in investing activities) with an effect of $0.5 billion; write offs of previously capitalised exploratory well costs are now added back within 'cash flow from operating activities' in "other" and not deducted from capital expenditure with an effect of $0.5 billion; and major inspection costs are capitalised (and therefore shown in "investing activities") and were previously expensed. This has an effect of $0.4 billion.*[5]

IFRS Example 2[6]:

(Millions of Euros)

For the 12 Months Ending Dec 31	2005	2004
Cash flow from operating activities		
Net profit for the period	29.6	3.2
Adjustments	41.7	65.5
Change in net working capital	0.2	0.2
Interest received	0.2	0.4
Interest paid	(25.7)	(25.4)
Other financial items	(0.3)	(0.9)
Dividends received	—	0.2
Taxes received/paid	0.8	(1.8)
Net cash generated by operating activities	46.5	41.4
Cash flow from investing activities		
Investments in investment properties	(53.1)	(57.5)
Investments in tangible and intangible assets	(0.2)	(0.3)
Proceeds from disposal of investment properties	9.2	37.6
Proceeds from disposal of tangible and intangible assets	0.2	—
Net cash used in investing activities	(43.9)	(20.2)
Cash flow from financing activities		
Increase in share capital related to use of convertible bond loans	1.6	1.6
Proceeds of long-term borrowings	100.0	250.0
Repayments of long-term borrowings	(75.7)	(260.7)
Proceeds/repayments of short-term borrowings	10.0	10.3
Dividends paid	(39.4)	(23.5)
Net cash generated from financing activities	(3.5)	(22.3)
Change in cash and cash equivalents	(0.9)	(1.1)
Cash and cash equivalents at Jan 1	1.7	2.8
Cash and cash equivalents at 31 Dec	0.8	1.7

Outlook for Convergence

Standards for the statement of cash flows are highly converged now between U.S. GAAP and IFRS. In fact, the U.S. Securities and Exchange Commission accepts statements of cash flows prepared under either SFAS No. 95 or IAS 7. Presently, the biggest discrepancies between the two sets of standards relate to the classification of certain cash flows, as shown in Exhibit 11.9. The joint FASB-IASB financial statement presentation project (see Chapter 13) will introduce a modified, converged classification scheme that will resolve such discrepancies.

Implications of Potential Changes

Convergence will result in more accurate and more comparable classifications of cash flows. Along the way, the concept of "cash equivalents" is virtually certain to be discarded, and therefore changes in such assets will no longer be included in statements of cash flows. And because a requirement to use the direct method of cash flow statement presentation would dramatically change current practice in the United States, financial managers should be vigilant for Convergence developments in this area.

Conclusion

This chapter reinforces an important truth about the FASB's and IASB's Convergence efforts: different Convergence projects can unfold in very different ways. But another important truth should now be apparent as well: several key measures of financial performance will be significantly affected by the process of Convergence.

Notes

1. Since 2002, respondents to the annual surveys conducted by the Financial Accounting Standards Advisory Council (FASAC), the FASB's primary advisory body, have consistently indicated that revenue recognition should be the FASB's top standard-setting priority. See www.fasb.org/fasac.
2. See, for example, Susan Scholz, *The Changing Nature and Consequences of Public Company Financial Restatements 1997–2006*, U.S. Department of the Treasury, April 2008.
3. Form 10-Q filed by Verizon Communications Inc. on May 4, 2007.
4. DaimlerChrysler AG "IFRS Consolidated Financial Statements as of December 31, 2006". Used by permission .
5. SEC Form 6-K filed by Royal Dutch Petroleum Co. on April 22, 2005.
6. Sponda Plc 2005 Annual Report.

CHAPTER 12

Business Combinations, Intercompany Investments, and Segment Reporting

This chapter summarizes the impact of Convergence on areas of financial accounting and reporting that involve relationships between and within business entities, including:

- Business combinations
- Intercompany investments
- Segment reporting

Business Combinations

Summary of Major Standards

Exhibits 12.1 and 12.2 show the major standards for business combinations under U.S. generally accepted accounting principles (GAAP) and International Financial Reporting Standards (IFRS), respectively.

Comparison of Standards

Exhibit 12.3 provides a comparison of major provisions of standards for business combinations between U.S. GAAP and IFRS.

Outlook for Convergence

In December 2007, upon issuing Statement of Financial Accounting Standards (SFAS) No. 141(R), *Business Combinations*, and SFAS No. 160,

EXHIBIT 12.1 Major Standards for Business Combinations under U.S. GAAP

Reference		Title	Last Revision
SFAS	141(R)	*Business Combinations*	Dec 2007
FIN	4	*Applicability of FASB Statement No. 2 to Business Combinations Accounted for by the Purchase Method*	Feb 1975 (superseded*)

* For annual reporting periods beginning on or after December 15, 2008.
See also FASB Codification Topic 805, *Business Combinations*.

EXHIBIT 12.2 Major Standards for Business Combinations under IFRS

Reference		Title	Last Revision
IFRS	3	*Business Combinations*	Jan 2008

Noncontrolling Interests in Consolidated Financial Statements (also covered in this chapter's "Intercompany Investments" section), the Financial Accounting Standards Board (FASB) announced that the issued statements represented "the completion of the FASB's first major joint project with the International Accounting Standards Board (IASB), as well as a significant convergence milestone."[1] The project referred to in the announcement was the boards' joint Convergence project on business combinations, which the boards undertook in cooperation with each other after having previously engaged in standard-setting work on business combinations independently of each other.

Given the announced completion of the joint business combinations Convergence project, one might conclude that U.S. GAAP and IFRS are converged in that area. But the reality is that there are many remaining differences between U.S. GAAP and IFRS in the area of business combinations. So what does the announcement about the "completion" of the joint project actually mean?

In this case, "close enough" seems to have been "good enough" for the FASB and IASB. After making concrete progress toward developing improved, converged standards for business combinations, the boards chose to stop working toward further standard-level Convergence in that area. The boards have, however, planned a post-implementation review of their standards in 2012.

Implications of Potential Changes

As a result of the "completion" of the FASB-IASB business combinations project, U.S. GAAP changed significantly in ways that brought it into closer conformity with current IFRS. And while IFRS changed as well, the changes were generally fewer and less significant than the changes to U.S. GAAP.

EXHIBIT 12.3   Comparison of Major Provisions of Standards for Business
Combinations, U.S. GAAP versus IFRS

	U.S. GAAP	IFRS
Acquisition ("Purchase") Method (i.e., for "Acquisitions")	Required	Required
Pooling of Interests Method (i.e., for "Mergers")	Prohibited	Prohibited
Special Treatment for Combinations of Entities under Common Control	Yes	No

Measurement of Acquisition Cost	■ Fair value of consideration given as of acquisition date
	  ■ **CURRENT:** Plus contingent consideration that is determinable in amount as of the date of acquisition
	  ■ **NEW*:** Including contingent consideration
	■ **CURRENT ONLY:** "Direct" out-of-pocket costs and expected nonobligatory restructuring costs
		■ Fair value of consideration given as of acquisition date
		  ■ **CURRENT:** Plus contingent consideration that is probable and can be measured reliably as of the date of acquisition
		  ■ **NEW**:** Including contingent consideration
		■ **CURRENT ONLY:** "Direct" out-of-pocket costs

Purchased In-Process Research & Development	**CURRENT:** Expensed immediately at fair value unless it has an alternative future use **NEW*:** May be recognized either as an acquired limited-life intangible asset or as part of goodwill if not separately measurable	May be recognized either as an acquired limited-life intangible asset or as part of goodwill if not separately measurable

(Continued)

EXHIBIT 12.3   *(Continued)*

	U.S. GAAP	IFRS
Goodwill	Excess of acquisition cost over the fair value of net identifiable assets acquired **CURRENT:** Proportionate method only **NEW*:** Full method only	Excess of acquisition cost over the fair value of net identifiable assets acquired **CURRENT:** Proportionate method only **NEW**:** Full or proportionate method
Negative Goodwill	**CURRENT:** Allocate excess on a pro rata basis to reduce the carrying amounts of certain acquired assets; recognize any remainder as extraordinary gain in profit/loss **NEW*:** Recognize as gain immediately in profit/loss	Recognize as gain immediately in profit/loss

* For annual reporting periods beginning on or after December 15, 2008.
** For annual reporting periods beginning on or after July 1, 2009.

Ironically, however, some of the changes to IFRS created new differences between IFRS and U.S. GAAP. For example, IFRS now allow acquiring entities their choice of using either the full or proportionate method of allocating goodwill between controlling and noncontrolling interests in situations where the acquirer obtains control of the acquiree without obtaining exclusive ownership. Additionally, IFRS do not require retrospective pro-forma disclosures of revenue and earnings of the combined entity as U.S. GAAP does. But given the FASB and IASB's recent decision to suspend work on Convergence in this area, there is currently no expected manner or time frame in which those kinds of differences will be eliminated.

Intercompany Investments

Summary of Major Standards

Exhibits 12.4 and 12.5 show the major standards for intercompany investments under U.S. GAAP and IFRS, respectively.

Comparison of Standards

Exhibit 12.6 provides a comparison of major provisions of standards for intercompany investments between U.S. GAAP and IFRS.

EXHIBIT 12.4 Major Standards for Intercompany Investments under U.S. GAAP

Reference		Title	Last Revision
ARB	51	*Consolidated Financial Statements (as amended)*	Aug 1959
APB Opinion	18	*The Equity Method of Accounting for Investments in Common Stock*	Mar 1971
SFAS	52	*Foreign Currency Translation*	Dec 1981
	94	*Consolidation of All Majority-owned Subsidiaries*	Oct 1987
	115	*Accounting for Certain Investments in Debt and Equity Securities*	May 1993
	140	*Accounting for Transfers and Servicing of Financial Assets and Extinguishments of Liabilities*	Sep 2000
	160	*Noncontrolling Interests in Consolidated Financial Statements*	Dec 2007
FIN	46(R)	*Consolidation of Variable Interest Entities*	Dec 2003

See also FASB Codification

- Topic 320, *Investments—Debt and Equity Securities*
- Topic 323, *Investments—Equity Method and Joint Ventures*
- Topic 810, *Consolidation*
- Subtopic 830-30, *Translation of Financial Statements*

EXHIBIT 12.5 Major Standards for Intercompany Investments under IFRS

Reference		Title	Last Revision
IAS	21	*The Effects of Changes in Foreign Exchange Rates*	Dec 2005
	27	*Consolidated and Separate Financial Statements*	Jan 2008
	28	*Investments in Associates*	Dec 2003
	31	*Interests In Joint Ventures*	Jan 2008
	39	*Financial Instruments: Recognition and Measurement*	May 2008
SIC	12	*Consolidation—Special Purpose Entities*	Nov 1998
	13	*Jointly Controlled Entities—Non-monetary Contributions by Venturers*	Nov 1998

EXHIBIT 12.6 Comparison of Major Provisions of Standards for Intercompany Investments, U.S. GAAP versus IFRS

	U.S. GAAP	IFRS
Investor Has No Influence over Investee	In general, fair value (fair value adjustments are taken into profit or loss)	In general, fair value (fair value adjustments are taken into profit or loss)
Investor Has Significant Influence but Not Control (Investor-Associate)	■ In general, presumed if investor holds 20% or more of the voting power ■ Equity method ■ No consolidation	■ In general, presumed if investor holds 20% or more of the voting power ■ Equity method ■ No consolidation
Single-Investor control (Parent-Subsidiary)	■ In general, presumed if investor holds more than 50 percent of the voting power ■ Consolidation	■ In general, presumed if Investor holds more than 50% of the voting power ■ Consolidation
Joint-Investor Control (Venturer-Joint Venture)	Equity method (without consolidation) required except in certain industries where proportionate consolidation is permitted	Either proportionate consolidation (preferred) **or** the equity method (without consolidation)
Variable Interest Entity (VIE)	Consolidation required if and only if Investor is the "primary beneficiary" of the VIE (determined using a "risks and rewards" model)	No specific guidance
Special Purpose Entity (SPE—a kind of VIE)	**If "qualifying":** Not consolidated **If not "qualifying":** Consolidate if and only if investor "controls" investee (in the case of a voting interest entity) or is the primary beneficiary of the investee (in the case of a VIE)	No special treatment

EXHIBIT 12.6 *(Continued)*

	U.S. GAAP	IFRS
Noncontrolling Interests in Investee Reported by Controlling Investor	**CURRENT:** ■ Non-controlling share in the equity of Investees is separately stated between liabilities and shareholders' equity ■ Non-controlling share in the income of Investees is presented as an expense in the consolidated income statement **NEW*:** ■ Noncontrolling share in the equity of investees is separately stated within shareholders' equity ■ Noncontrolling share in the income of investees is separately stated in the consolidated income statement	■ Noncontrolling share in the equity of Investees is separately stated within shareholders' equity ■ Noncontrolling share in the income of Investees is separately stated in the consolidated income statement
Investees' Financial Statements—Foreign Currency Translation	■ Use the current rate method to translate from the investee's functional currency into the Investor's presentation currency ■ Foreign currency translation adjustments are recognized as a separate component of equity (and are therefore included in Other Comprehensive Income)	■ Use the current rate method to translate from the investee's functional currency into the Investor's presentation currency ■ Foreign currency translation adjustments are recognized as a separate component of equity (and are therefore included in Other Comprehensive Income)

* For annual reporting periods beginning on or after December 15, 2008.

Note: Under the current rate method, the exchange rate as of the balance sheet date is used to translate assets and liabilities; shareholders' equity is translated at historical rates; revenues and expenses are translated at exchange rates as of the dates of the transactions/events (or at average exchange rates for a period).

Examples of How Standards Are Applied in Practice

The following excerpts from notes to actual financial statements illustrate how standards for intercompany investments are commonly applied in practice under U.S. GAAP and IFRS.

> *Transition from U.K. GAAP to IFRS: Under IFRS, the legal and contractual power to control or significantly influence is the key consideration when determining whether an entity is a subsidiary, joint venture or associate. Under UK GAAP, consideration was given to the control or significant influence actually exercised in practice when making this decision. A review of investments concluded that the group's beer interests in Malaysia and Singapore, classified as subsidiaries under UK GAAP, should be classified as jointly controlled entities under IFRS. As a consequence, these entities previously fully consolidated (with a minority interest) under UK GAAP are proportionately consolidated under IFRS. This adjustment did not affect the retained profit of the group. . . . For all proportionately consolidated entities, the IFRS balance sheet includes only the group's share of the assets and liabilities of those entities. Where an entity was previously fully consolidated under UK GAAP, the minority interest portion does not exist under IFRS. The overall impact for the year ended 30 June 2005 was a reduction in sales of £41 million and operating profit of £8 million. The group's net assets at 30 June 2005 were reduced by £26 million due to the change in minority interests (1 July 2004—£24 million), but the equity attributable to equity shareholders of the parent company was not affected."[2]*

IFRS[3]:

(Millions of Euros)

For the 12 Months Ending Dec 31	2006
Revenues	152,809
Cost of sales	(126,137)
Gross profit	26,672
Selling expenses	(11,519)
General administrative expenses	(5,989)
Research and noncapitalized development costs	(4,228)
Other operating income, net	777
Share of profit (loss) from companies accounted for using the equity method, net	(150)
Other financial income (expense), net	(74)
Earnings before interest and taxes (EBIT)	5,489

IFRS *(Continued)*

For the 12 Months Ending Dec 31	2006
Earnings before interest and taxes (EBIT)	5,489
Interest expense, net	(401)
Profit before income taxes	5,088
Income tax expense	(1,305)
Net profit	3,783
Minority interest	(39)
Profit attributable to shareholders of DaimlerChrysler AG	3,744

U.S. GAAP[4]:

(Thousands of U.S. Dollars)

For the First Quarter	2007	2006
Sales	2,436,253	2,423,537
Cost of goods sold and occupancy costs	1,813,029	1,796,783
Gross profit	623,224	626,754
Operating and other expenses:		
Operating and selling	420,768	433,045
General and administrative	93,937	89,233
Other operating (income) expense, net	(1,576)	112,840
Operating income (loss)	110,095	(8,364)
Other income (expense):		
Interest expense	(30,116)	(31,503)
Interest income	23,037	21,114
Other expense, net	(3,447)	(2,166)
Income (loss) from continuing operations before income taxes and minority interest	99,569	(20,919)
Income tax expense	(38,832)	7,994
Income (loss) from continuing operations before minority interest	60,737	(12,925)
Minority interest, net of income tax	(2,198)	(1,181)
Income (loss) from continuing operations	58,539	(14,106)

(Continued)

U.S. GAAP *(Continued)*

For the First Quarter	2007	2006
Income (loss) from continuing operations	58,539	(14,106)
Discontinued operations:		
Operating loss	—	(17,972)
Income tax benefit	—	6,991
Loss from discontinued operations	—	(10,981)
Net income (loss)	58,539	(25,087)
Preferred dividends	(1,008)	(1,009)
Net income (loss) applicable to common shareholders	57,531	(26,096)

Canadian entity using U.S. GAAP: *The US dollar is the functional currency for most of the Company's worldwide operations. For foreign operations where the local currency is the functional currency, specifically the Company's Canadian operations, assets and liabilities denominated in foreign currencies are translated into US dollars at end-of-period exchange rates, and the resultant translation adjustments are reported, net of their related tax effects, as a component of Accumulated Other Comprehensive Income in Stockholders' Equity.... Income and expenses are translated into US dollars at the average exchange rates in effect during the period.[5]*

Outlook for Convergence

Many aspects of financial accounting and reporting for intercompany investments are substantially converged between current U.S. GAAP and current IFRS. Nevertheless, for many years the FASB and IASB have engaged in loosely coupled efforts to improve their current standards in this area as well as to converge the unconverged aspects of their standards.

Much of the boards' standard-setting work on inter-company investments relates directly to the concept of the *reporting entity* as addressed in Phase D of the joint conceptual framework project (see Chapter 4). The central issue is "Under what circumstances should potentially separate reporting entities prepare financial statements on a consolidated basis?" The boards' conclusion: it's all about *control*, that is, when one entity has control over another. However, the boards continue to debate what exactly constitutes control in the case of inter-company investments.

Stakeholders in the financial reporting supply chain, including the Securities and Exchange Commission (SEC), have put increasing pressure on the FASB and IASB to pursue improvements and Convergence more aggressively in this area. In particular, the financial accounting and reporting treatment of *special purpose entities* (SPEs) and other *variable interest entities* (VIEs) has become a significant concern in the wake of past corporate scandals (such as Enron) and the recent turmoil in the world's credit markets.

In response, the FASB has focused on several specific issues, the most prominent of which is whether transferors of financial assets to SPEs should prepare financial statements that present the transferor and its SPEs as a consolidated reporting entity. The FASB has actually had a "Transfers of Financial Assets" project on its agenda for more than five years. But while the project relates to work currently being done by the IASB, it is not, strictly speaking, a joint Convergence project with the IASB.

The overall purpose of the "Transfers of Financial Assets" project is to simplify the guidance on accounting for transfers of financial assets as found in SFAS No. 140. The project is also being performed in conjunction with another FASB-only project on the reconsideration of FASB Interpretation (FIN) 46(R). Of particular interest to the FASB and its constituents are *qualifying* SPE (QSPEs), which have "allowed banks and other entities to keep mortgage-backed securities and other passive investment vehicles that are legally isolated from the banks that created them, off their books"[6] as a result of the guidance of QSPEs under SFAS No. 140 and FIN 46(R)—guidance that, in practice, almost always results in nonconsolidation. The FASB has noted that:

> *Constituents have voiced concerns over the lack of transparency (either through consolidation or disclosure) of the enterprises' involvement with structures that contained significant risk; for example, they cite an inability to understand the nature of the enterprises' involvement and maximum exposure and an inability to assess the current status of their exposure.*[7]

Among several planned improvements to U.S. GAAP, the FASB has decided to remove the concept of a QSPE from SFAS No. 140 and to remove the scope exception for QSPEs from FIN 46(R).[8] Additionally, the determination of whether or not to consolidate a VIE (including SPEs) under FIN 46(R) will become more qualitative and less quantitative in nature.

Due process toward the finalization of amendments to SFAS No. 140 and FIN 46(R) is proceeding apace as of mid-2008. In the meantime, the FASB and IASB are also jointly conducting a research project on consolidations in general, with the IASB taking the lead on standard-setting work and the FASB monitoring that work. In 2008, the IASB is expected to issue a consultative document on its work, "at which time the FASB will consider whether to issue an Invitation to Comment based on the IASB document."[9]

Looking further ahead, another potential change to watch for is that the proportional consolidation method may be eradicated from future converged standards.

Implications of Potential Changes

The FASB's proposed amendments to SFAS No. 140 and FIN 46(R) will undoubtedly have a major impact on the financial statements of companies that have created or are otherwise associated with QSPEs, as is common in the financial services industry. "[V]ariable interest entities, previously accounted for as qualifying SPEs in Statement 140, will need to be analyzed for consolidation according to Interpretation 46(R)."[10] The FASB itself has warned that "the consolidation of QSPEs...may require massive consolidation of financial assets and liabilities."[11]

Of course, the underlying rationale for such changes is to make an entity's risk exposure more apparent users of the entity's financial statements. And given the disruptions to the global economy that have been blamed in part on a lack of transparency about risk exposure, the coming changes must be viewed as highly beneficial for financial statement users.

Segment Reporting

Summary of Major Standards

Exhibits 12.7 and 12.8 show the major standards for segment reporting under U.S. GAAP and IFRS, respectively.

Comparison of Standards

Exhibit 12.9 provides a comparison of major provisions of standards for segment reporting between U.S. GAAP and IFRS.

EXHIBIT 12.7   Major Standards for Segment Reporting under U.S. GAAP

Reference		Title	Last Revision
SFAS	131	*Disclosures about Segments of an Enterprise and Related Information*	Jun 1997

See also FASB Codification Topic 280, *Segment Reporting*.

EXHIBIT 12.8   Major Standards for Segment Reporting under IFRS

Reference		Title	Last Revision
IAS	14	*Segment Reporting* (fiscal years beginning before 2009)	Aug 1997
IFRS	8	*Operating Segments* (fiscal years beginning after 2008; early application encouraged)	Nov 2006

EXHIBIT 12.9   Comparison of Major Provisions of Standards for Segment Reporting, U.S. GAAP versus IFRS

	U.S. GAAP	IFRS
Segment Definition	Management approach	**CURRENT:** Management approach that identifies both "business" and "geographic" segments and determines which dimension is primary and which is secondary **NEW:** "Pure" management approach
Reportability Threshold	Based on a set of "10%" tests	**CURRENT and NEW:** Based on a set of "10%" tests
Vertically Integrated Segments	Disclosure required if reportability criteria are satisfied	**CURRENT:** Disclosure encouraged but not required if reportability criteria are satisfied **NEW:** Disclosure required if reportability criteria are satisfied
Accounting policies for reported segments	As used internally	**CURRENT:** Must be same as are used in consolidated reports **NEW:** As used internally
Interim reporting	Limited	**CURRENT:** Limited **NEW:** Significantly expanded

Examples of How Standards Are Applied in Practice

The following excerpts from notes to actual financial statements illustrate how standards for segment reporting are commonly applied in practice under U.S. GAAP and IFRS.

U.S. GAAP[12]:

(Millions of U.S. Dollars)

For the First Quarter	2006
Net sales:	
Electronics and Communications	202.0
Systems Engineering Solutions	68.9
Aerospace Engines and Components	53.1
Energy Systems	6.2
Total net sales	330.2
Operating profit and other segment income:	
Electronics and Communications	23.2
Systems Engineering Solutions	5.9
Aerospace Engines and Components	6.3
Energy Systems	—
Segment operating profit and other segment income	35.4
Corporate expense	(6.6)
Other income, net	1.0
Interest expense, net	(1.1)
Income before income taxes	28.7
Provision for income taxes	10.8
Net income	17.9

IFRS (per IAS 14): *The presentation of specific data from the consolidated financial statements is classified by divisions and geography. The primary reporting format is based on the corporate divisions.... The secondary reporting format is based on geography...."*[13]

(See also the tables that follow.)

Primary Segmentation—Results (Millions of Euros)

Year Ending Dec 31, 2006	Express	Mail	Inter-Company	Non-Allocated	Total
Net sales	5,922	4,025		1	9,948
Intercompany sales	9	8	(17)		
Other operating revenues	80	32			112

Primary Segmentation—Results (Millions of Euros) *(Continued)*

Year Ending Dec 31, 2006	Express	Mail	Inter-Company	Non-Allocated	Total
Total operating revenues	6,011	4,065	(17)	1	10,060
Other income	6	58		1	65
Depreciation/impairment PP&E	(142)	(107)		(6)	(255)
Amortization/impairment intangibles	(34)	(28)		(1)	(63)
Total operating income	580	761		(65)	1,276
Net financial income/(expense)					(47)
Results from investments in associates					(6)
Income tax					(395)
Profit/(loss) from discontinued operations					(157)
Profit for the year					671
Attributable to:					
Minority interests					1
Equity holders of the parent					670

Secondary Segments—Geographical
(Millions of Euros)

Year Ending Dec 31	2006
Europe	
The Netherlands	3,633
United Kingdom	1,349
Italy	774
Germany	950
France	649
Belgium	277
Rest of Europe	1,130

(Continued)

Secondary Segments—Geographical
(Continued)

Year Ending Dec 31	2006
Americas	
USA and Canada	74
South and Middle America	43
Africa and the Middle East	89
Australia and Pacific	442
Asia	
China and Taiwan	288
India	51
Rest of Asia	199
Total net sales	9,948

Outlook for Convergence

Convergence in the area of segment reporting is a rare case of the IASB having recently adopted a major U.S. GAAP standard essentially word-for-word in its entirety. The board's decision represents one of the most notable examples of "pure" unilateral standard-level Convergence in recent years. But that decision provoked political outcry in the European Union largely because it was viewed as a direct importation of U.S. GAAP without regard for the effect on European constituents of the IASB.

In November 2007, the European Parliament adopted a resolution[14] grudgingly accepting the European Commission's (EC's) endorsement of IFRS 8. The resolution was highly critical of the IASB's actions with regard to promulgating that standard, even going so far as to preach that "convergence of accounting rules is not a one-sided process where one party simply copies the financial reporting standards of the other party." Of course, unilateral standard-level Convergence is not the only way Convergence can happen, but sometimes it is the way that Convergence should and does happen.

As discussed in Chapter 1, many individuals in the United States who oppose IFRS and its growing influence on U.S. GAAP do so for invalid reasons. One of the leading lines of "reasoning" is that IFRS should be rejected because they are "foreign" and therefore inferior to U.S. GAAP. It is therefore enlightening, if not consoling, to realize that in much of Europe and elsewhere in the world, the IASB is wrongly viewed as a puppet of U.S. interests and that IFRS are viewed as deteriorating in quality as a result of becoming increasingly "Americanized." If success at Convergence means that converged standards are equally offensive to everyone, we are well on our way.

The political controversy over IFRS 8 reinforces the continued existence a significant threat to attaining the goal of Convergence—the threat that governmental interference in the process of setting financial reporting standards could lead to individual jurisdictions overriding the actions of a country-neutral standard setter. This has already happened in Europe and elsewhere in the world, for example, with the EC's "carve out" of certain provisions of IAS 39. "Jurisidictionalism" may in fact be the leading threat to Convergence, and we are currently far from eliminating or mitigating its effects.

Implications of Potential Changes

One of the thorniest issues in segment reporting under U.S. GAAP, and now IFRS, is that comparability across entities may be quite low. This is the result of segment reporting under current standards being based on "management's view" of the entity and its business. Because the management of one entity may view the entity differently from the management of another entity that is virtually identical to the first, considerable diversity in segment reporting can and does happen in practice. So while segment reporting standards are converged at this time, they may still be subject to ongoing improvement directed at enhancing comparability.

Conclusion

The areas of financial accounting and reporting covered in the chapter demonstrate that standard-setting priorities can shift quickly. Major projects can end abruptly, while "back-burner" projects can heat up just as abruptly due to changes in economy on a national or global level.

This chapter's topics also illustrate how standard setting can influence and be influenced by political activity. It is helpful to remember that the relationship between politics and financial reporting can never truly be severed because politics is ultimately about economics—and so is financial reporting.

Notes

1. Financial Accounting Standards Board, press release, "FASB Issues FASB Statements No. 141 (R), *Business Combinations* and No. 160, *Noncontrolling Interests in Consolidated Financial Statements*," December 4, 2007.

2. SEC Form 20-F filed by Diageo Plc on September 25, 2006.
3. DaimlerChrysler AG "IFRS Consolidated Financial Statements as of December 31, 2006." Used by permission.
4. SEC Form 10-Q filed by OfficeMax Incorporated on May 7, 2007. Used by permission.
5. SEC Form 10-K filed by Tesco Corp. on March 29, 2007.
6. AccountingWEB, Inc., "FASB will add disclosure requirements to Statement 140" [online], June 5, 2008 [accessed July 5, 2008], available at www.accountingweb.com/cgi-bin/item.cgi?id=105295.
7. Financial Accounting Standards Board, project update, "Reconsideration of FIN 46(R) Consolidation of Variable Interest Entities" [online], June 18, 2008 [accessed July 5, 2008], available at www.fasb.org/project/reconsideration_fin46r.shtml.
8. Financial Accounting Standards Board, project update, "Transfers of Financial Assets" [online], June 18, 2008 [accessed July 5, 2008], available at www.fasb.org/project/transfers_of_financial_assets.shtml.
9. Financial Accounting Standards Board, research projects, "Consolidations: Policy and Procedure" [online], March 13, 2008 [accessed July 5, 2008], available at www.fasb.org/project/research_projects.shtml#consolidations.
10. See note 8.
11. See note 7.
12. SEC Form 10-Q filed by Teledyne Technologies Incorporated on May 8, 2006. Used by permission.
13. TNT N.V. 2006 Annual Report. Used by permission.
14. European Parliament, adopted text P6_TA(2007)0526, "Resolution of 14 November 2007 on the Draft Commission Regulation Amending Regulation (EC) No 1725/2003 Adopting Certain International Accounting Standards in Accordance with Regulation (EC) No 1606/2002 of the European Parliament and of the Council as Regards International Financial Reporting Standard (IFRS) 8, Concerning Disclosure of Operating Segments."

CHAPTER 13

Financial Statements: What Is Ahead

This chapter concludes Part Three's examination of the impact of Convergence on financial reporting in the United States by focusing on how the contents and formats of the principal financial statements will change as U.S. generally accepted accounting principles (GAAP) and International Financial Reporting Standards (IFRS) converge. The anticipated changes will represent the most visible—and possibly the most controversial—effects of Convergence in the U.S. financial reporting supply chain.

Financial Statement Presentation Project

For several years, the Financial Accounting Standards Board (FASB) has been working jointly with the International Accounting Standards Board (IASB) on a project that will dramatically change the contents and formats of the principal financial statements. Far more than just a cosmetic makeover, the Financial Statement Presentation project aims to overhaul the principal financial statements in ways that are intended to enhance their understandability and usefulness to investors, creditors, and other financial statement users.

As Convergence eliminates differences between U.S. GAAP and IFRS, each set of standards will undergo profound changes because the FASB and IASB are dedicated to improving current standards as well as converging them—and opportunities for improvement are plentiful. But not all of the changes that the boards have proposed for the financial statements have been welcomed by preparers, auditors, regulators, and users in the U.S. financial reporting supply chain.

Objective and Scope

The objective of the Financial Statement Presentation project is:

> *[T]o establish a common, high-quality standard for presentation of information in the individual financial statements (and among the financial statements) that will improve the ability of investors, creditors, and other financial statement users to:*

> - *Understand an entity's present and past financial position*
> - *Understand the past operating, financing, and other activities that caused an entity's financial position to change and the components of those changes*
> - *Use that financial statement information (along with information from other sources) to assess the amounts, timing, and uncertainty of an entity's future cash flows.*[1]

The scope of the project encompasses all business entities, both public and private, but will not apply to nonbusiness entities (i.e., not-for-profit organizations or defined-benefit plans).[2] Private companies, however, have expressed concerns about being included in the scope of the project. For example, in a letter to the FASB, the Private Company Financial Reporting Committee raised the possibility of private companies being exempt from the standards that are expected to result from the project.[3]

The Financial Statement Presentation project has been organized into three phases (A, B, and C), which are described in the following subsections.

Phase A

Phase A of the Financial Statement Presentation is essentially complete. It addressed what constitutes a complete set of financial statements and the requirements for presenting comparative financial information.

The FASB and IASB agreed that a complete set of financial statements for each reporting period should consist of:

- A Statement of Financial Position as of the beginning of the reporting period, which shows balances of assets, liabilities, and equity
- A Statement of Financial Position as of the end of the reporting period
- A Statement of Comprehensive Income, which shows, for the reporting period, the changes in assets and liabilities other than those arising from transactions with owners in their capacity as owners

- A Statement of Changes in Equity, which shows the changes in assets and liabilities arising from transactions with owners in their capacity as owners, along with the total net effect of comprehensive income
- A Statement of Cash Flows, which shows inflows and outflows of cash

The boards also decided to require presentation of comparative information consisting of, at a minimum, a complete set of financial statements for two annual periods (i.e., the current and prior annual periods). While these changes do not represent a significant departure from current practice, the contents and formats of the individual statements will be very different from what they are today mainly as a result of the project's next phase.

Phase B

Phase B of the Financial Statement Presentation project addresses fundamental issues of presenting information in the financial statements. Those issues include:

- Classification and display of line items in each financial statement
- Principles for aggregating and disaggregating information in each financial statement
- Defining the totals and subtotals to be reported in each financial statement
- Use of the direct method versus the indirect method in preparing the Statement of Cash Flows

In October 2008, the FASB and IASB issued a discussion paper (DP) containing their preliminary views on Phase B issues. The DP describes a set of objectives for financial statement presentation. The objectives specify that information should be presented in the financial statements in a manner that:

- Portrays a cohesive financial picture of an entity's activities.
- Disaggregates information so that it is useful in predicting an entity's future cash flows.
- Helps users assess an entity's liquidity and financial flexibility.

The DP for Phase B also contains proposed formats for the financial statements (see Exhibit 13.1). Under the proposed formats, much of the traditional organization of today's financial statements would be swept away. With the exception of the Statement of Changes in Equity, for which no changes have been proposed, the boards have proposed that each of the

EXHIBIT 13.1   Working Format for Presenting Information within the Financial
Statements

Statement of Financial Position	Statement of Comprehensive Income	Statement of Cash Flows
Business ■ Operating assets and liabilities ■ Investing assets and liabilities	Business ■ Operating income and expenses ■ Investing income and expenses	Business ■ Operating cash flows ■ Investing cash flows
Financing ■ Financing assets ■ Financing liabilities	Financing ■ Financing asset income ■ Financing liability expenses	Financing ■ Financing asset cash flows ■ Financing liability cash flows
Income Taxes	Income Taxes on continuing operations (business and financing activities)	Income Taxes
Discontinued Operations	Discontinued Operations, Net of Tax	Discontinued Operations
Equity	Other Comprehensive Income, Net of Tax	Equity

Source: Financial Accounting Standards Board, Discussion Paper, *Preliminary Views on Financial Statement Presentation*, October 16, 2008. Copyright © 2008 by Financial Accounting Standards Board, 401 Merritt 7, PO Box 5116, Norwalk, CT 06856. All rights reserved. Used by permission.

principal financial statements be organized into the same parallel sections, reflecting new groupings of items.

Because the new statements are based on a novel manner of classifying financial statement items, here are few things to note about classification:

■ The Business, Financing, and Income Taxes sections relate to continuing operations, in contrast to the Discontinued Operations section.
■ The Business section of the statements relates to the entity's value-creation activities and is intended to be disaggregated into Operating and Investing categories. The Operating category is intended for assets and liabilities (and changes in those assets and liabilities) that management views as related to the central purpose(s) for which the entity is in business. The Investing category is intended to include assets and liabilities (and any changes in those assets and liabilities) that management views as unrelated to the central purpose for which the entity is in business.

- The Financing section is intended to be disaggregated into asset and liability categories, reflecting assets and liabilities (and any changes in those assets and liabilities) that management views as part of the financing of the entity's business activities but are independent of specific business activities and do not involve transactions with owners.
- Gains and losses on transactions in foreign currency, including the components of any net gain or loss on remeasuring the financial statements of an entity into its functional currency, would be included in the same section and category as the assets/liabilities that gave rise to the gains/losses.
- The FASB and IASB have not yet reached a conclusion on how "basket" transactions should or should not be allocated among sections/categories.

In particular, the Statement of Financial Position would no longer be organized into the traditional asset, liability, and equity sections. However, entities would be required to disclose total assets and total liabilities either on the face of the statement or in the accompanying notes. Additionally, entities would generally be required to present assets and liabilities in short- and long-term subcategories and would be expected to disclose totals for short-term assets, short-term liabilities, long-term assets, and long-term liabilities.

With regard to the Statement of Cash Flows, the introduction of separate Income Taxes, Discontinued Operations, and Equity sections represents a significant departure from current practice. And as seen in the DP, the FASB and IASB are inclined to require the use of the direct method of preparing the Statement of Cash Flows; that method is currently permissible and in fact recommended by the FASB, although it is not commonly used in practice. Despite protests from a minority of preparers who claim to be unable to produce a direct-method Statement of Cash Flows, such statements are generally considered to be easier to understand and more decision-useful than statements prepared under the indirect method.

The proposed Statement of Comprehensive Income provides multiple performance measures of greater distinction and detail than those found in today's income statements. Within the sections and categories of the proposed Statement of Comprehensive Income, functional line items will detail sales revenue, cost-of-sales expense, marketing expenses, and so forth. A functional line item may be further disaggregated by nature (e.g., labor, materials, depreciation, etc.), either on the face of the statement or in the accompanying notes. Any other significant item of income or expense (e.g., goodwill impairment) would be stated separately within the appropriate category/section.

Although there is widespread support for a single statement that includes all items of comprehensive income as proposed in the DP, the FASB and IASB have made it clear that they intend to eventually eliminate the distinction between "Net Income" items and "Other Comprehensive Income" (OCI) items[4] and possibly even leave the income statement with no single "bottom-line" figure summarizing financial performance.[5] This has led to considerable controversy. In particular, the potential elimination of net income as a reported measure has many observers worried.[6] But for now, the boards have proposed to:

- Continue to require the disclosure of net income
- Require the presentation of OCI items in a separate section of the Statement of Comprehensive Income
- Require disclosure of the category (i.e., operating, investing, or financing) to which each OCI item relates

The preservation of OCI also means that "recycling" of items from OCI to net income will continue to occur.

Another controversial element of the Phase B proposal is the requirement for reporting entities to present a new columnar schedule that reconciles the Statement of Cash Flows to the Statement of Comprehensive Income. Starting with the Business, Financing, Income Taxes, and Discontinued Operations sections of the Statement of Cash Flows (keeping in mind that the Statement of Cash Flows will have been prepared using the direct method), adjustments are then recognized for:

- Accruals, systematic allocations, and other changes that are not remeasurements (e.g., depreciation, capital expenditures, noncash interest expense)
- Remeasurements that represent recurring changes in fair value (e.g., unrealized holding gains/losses on trading securities)
- Remeasurements other than recurring changes in fair value (e.g., impairment losses)

The cash-flow items, as adjusted, should then tie to the corresponding sections of the Statement of Comprehensive Income.

Preliminary field testing of the financial statement presentation model proposed in the DP will be conducted throughout the document's comment period, which ends April 14, 2009. Interestingly, while the IASB has indicated that the proposed changes would not apply to entities that lack public accountability, the FASB states in the DP that they have "not considered explicitly whether the proposals in this Discussion Paper would apply to nonpublic entities." Thus, the ultimate entity scope may or may not include nonpublic entities.

Phase C

Phase C of the Financial Statement Presentation project will address interim reporting. Topics to be deliberated by the FASB and IASB in this phase include:

- The financial statements to be included in an interim financial report
- Whether "condensed" formats for financial statements in an interim financial report should be allowed
- What comparative periods, if any, should be required or allowed in interim financial reports

As of late 2008, this phase had not yet commenced.

Other Financial Statement Issues

It has been claimed by some observers that the growing use of eXtensible Business Reporting Language (XBRL) as a format for exchanging and storing financial information will render formal, standardized financial statements obsolete. The reality is that financial statements are likely to enjoy a long, useful life, as not all users will have the sophistication to "slice and dice" XBRL data to the extent that interactive data applications will eventually make possible. However, Convergence will certainly keep the XBRL organizations for both U.S. GAAP and IFRS very busy as standards change.

Currently, under U.S. GAAP, we have four pages of financial statements and what seems like 40—or even 400—pages of notes containing required disclosures. That situation is likely to change as a result of Convergence, but, unfortunately, in a way that will only add to the disclosures that are currently required under U.S. GAAP. Standard setters can always think of something else that reporting entities ought to tell financial statement users.

Conclusion

Convergence is bringing plenty of change to the contents and formats of the financial statements that flow through the financial reporting supply chain. In particular, the FASB and IASB's joint Financial Statement Presentation project is sure to influence all parties in the supply chain for years to come.

Notes

1. Financial Accounting Standards Board, project update, "Financial Statement Presentation—Joint Project of the IASB and FASB" [online], July 1, 2008 [accessed September 1, 2008], available at www.fasb.org/project/financial_statement_presentation.shtml.
2. Ibid.
3. Judith H. O'Dell, for the Private Company Financial Reporting Committee, letter about Financial Statement Presentation project, February 8, 2008, available at www.pcfr.org/downloads/PCFRC_final_letter_to_FASB_on_F-S_Presention_project_-_2-8-08_sent_to_FASB.pdf.
4. OCI items currently include (but are not limited to) unrealized holding gains/losses on "Available for Sale" securities; foreign currency translation adjustments; and losses from the recognition of a minimum liability arising from employer-sponsored defined-benefit plans.
5. This sentiment is not new on the FASB's part. Statement of Financial Accounting Concepts No. 5 (issued December 1984) states that the FASB "believes that it is important to avoid focusing attention almost exclusively on 'the bottom line,' earnings per share, or other highly simplified condensations."
6. See, for example, David Reilly, "Profit Could Be Lost with New Accounting Statements" [online], May 12, 2007, available at http://online.wsj.com/article/SB117893520139500814.html.

Part II Epilogue

This Part examined in detail how Convergence will impact financial reporting in the United States. As you have seen, virtually every aspect of preparing financial reports under both U.S. GAAP and IFRS will change as a result of Convergence.

Remember, the differences between current U.S. GAAP and current IFRS will matter to some companies, but they will not matter to most companies. What will matter to *all* companies that use U.S. GAAP now is how the financial reporting standards that will be used in the United States in the future will differ from current U.S. GAAP. And those changes are coming at an accelerating pace.

Thus, Convergence will challenge the individuals and institutions in the U.S. financial reporting supply chain to be something that they are not now—agile. U.S. financial professionals are a part of the lack-of-agility problem. The ultimate issue is who among us is willing to make the necessary plans and decisions—and to take the necessary actions—to become part of the solution.

Now that you have a better understanding of how Convergence is changing the technical aspects of financial reporting, you are ready for Part Three to explain how Convergence will impact the livelihoods of financial professionals in the United States and throughout the world.

PART III

Impact of Convergence on U.S. Labor Markets

As noted in Chapter 2, upheaval in U.S. labor markets can be expected as a result of Convergence. The chapters in this part will examine the specific ways in which Convergence will impact U.S. labor markets for financial reporting talent.

This part begins with Chapter 14 providing a current overview of U.S. labor markets for financial reporting talent. Then Chapters 15 through 18 will each address a different aspect of the coming impact, describing how Convergence will:

- Obsolesce the knowledge, skills, and abilities of financial professionals
- Commoditize financial reporting talent
- Globalize the supply of and demand for financial reporting talent
- Transform the talent supply pipeline

CHAPTER 14

Overview of U.S. Labor Markets for Financial Reporting Talent

The purpose of this chapter is to describe three defining characteristics of U.S. labor markets for financial reporting talent. Understanding the characteristics described in this chapter will help you better understand how and why Convergence will impact U.S. labor markets. Details of the "how and why" will be addressed in subsequent chapters.

The market characteristics that will be described in this chapter are:

- The geographic scope of supply and demand
- The role of U.S. generally accepted accounting principles (GAAP) in defining the "product"
- The nature of the talent supply "pipeline"

As you read about these characteristics, keep in mind that while each represents a distinct aspect of U.S. labor markets for financial reporting talent, the characteristics strongly interrelate with each other.

Geographic Scope of Supply and Demand

Traditionally, labor markets for financial reporting talent have not been global in scope. Political and cultural barriers that exist among countries have effectively segregated the supply of and demand for financial reporting talent into numerous distinct, country-specific labor markets. For example, U.S. labor markets are largely isolated from other countries' labor markets as a result of federal employment laws that significantly restrict who is entitled to work in the United States, as well as the dominance of English as the language of commerce in general and of financial reporting in particular.

Even within individual countries, there are typically many distinct labor markets for financial reporting talent that each exhibit a relatively high degree of geographic specificity. This has certainly been true in the United States, where labor markets have tended to be local or regional in scope rather than national.

Two factors are responsible for the narrow geographic scope of U.S. labor markets for financial reporting talent. First, U.S. employers have strongly preferred that employees be physically present at a specific place of work at specific times in order to facilitate supervision, collaboration, and the exchange of paper documents and other work products. Thus, the geographic scope of most labor markets has effectively been limited by commuting distance. Second, for many licensed professionals such as certified public accountants, licensure requirements and the right to practice have traditionally been state specific rather than national. The result has been relatively low international and interstate mobility among such professionals.

Role of U.S. GAAP

Independently of the legal, linguistic, and physical constraints on the geographic scope of supply and demand, U.S. labor markets for financial reporting talent have developed around a "product" that is highly differentiated from what is bought and sold in other countries' labor markets. With regard to financial reporting, the country-specific nature of the knowledge, skills, and abilities (KSAs) that employers demand has reinforced the narrow geographic scope of labor markets. Consequently,

- There is relatively limited availability of workers outside of the United States who, as a result of education and experience, possess the financial reporting KSAs that U.S. employers seek.
- There is relatively limited need among non-U.S. employers for the financial reporting KSAs that U.S. workers possess.

The country specificity of financial reporting KSAs in the United States and other countries has resulted directly from the country specificity of the financial reporting standards that are used in each country. Of course, in the United States, U.S. GAAP is by far the most commonly used set of financial reporting standards. Not surprisingly, then, the KSAs around which U.S. labor markets for financial reporting talent revolve have been heavily influenced by the distinctive characteristics of U.S. GAAP.

Talent Supply Pipeline

The "product" that is sold in U.S. markets for financial reporting talent (i.e., the labor of workers having the financial reporting KSAs demanded by employers) can be thought of as being supplied to the markets via a "pipeline." The pipeline of financial reporting talent in the United States consists of the individuals, institutions, and activities that collectively supply financial reporting talent to U.S. labor markets. Similar but separate supply pipelines exist in other countries that have labor markets for financial reporting talent.

In each country, it is the supply pipeline that ultimately determines the quantity and quality of financial reporting talent available to employers. In most countries, however, the operation of the financial reporting talent pipeline is predicated on a high degree of quantitative and qualitative stability in the demand for the KSAs that are bought and sold in labor markets. The financial reporting talent pipeline in the United States is a prime example of one that is essentially incapable of proactive change in anticipation of changes in market demand for KSAs, as well as one that lacks the agility to quickly undertake reactive change in response to changes in demand.

Conclusion

As described in this chapter, the supply of and demand for financial reporting talent in U.S. labor markets are shaped by various factors. U.S. labor markets for financial reporting talent can be characterized as being:

- Very limited in geographic scope
- Focused on country-specific KSAs
- Supplied by a pipeline that, at best, responds slowly to changing demand

As the remaining chapters of Part Three will explain, Convergence will profoundly change each of these characteristics, creating new managerial and personal challenges for all participants in U.S. labor markets for financial reporting talent.

CHAPTER 15

Obsolescence of Knowledge, Skills, and Abilities

Convergence will result in profound, fundamental changes to the knowledge, skills, and abilities (KSAs) that companies demand from workers. Specifically, many of the financial reporting KSAs now possessed by workers in U.S. labor markets will be rendered obsolete by Convergence. This chapter focuses on the obsolescence of workers' existing KSAs as one of four significant effects that Convergence will have on U.S. labor markets. The other three will be addressed in Chapters 16 through 18.

There are many reasons why Convergence will change the demand for financial reporting KSAs in U.S. labor markets, and it is important to recognize that the changes will be both quantitative and qualitative in nature. Furthermore, the obsolescence of existing financial reporting KSAs will be accompanied by short-term imbalances in the supply of and demand for financial reporting talent in U.S. labor markets. Each of those topics will now be examined in detail.

Why Demand Will Change

Throughout the world's labor markets, employers' demand for KSAs based on country-specific financial reporting standards is shrinking as a result of Convergence. Specifically in U.S. labor markets, where the KSAs that are bought and sold are currently based on U.S. generally accepted accounting principles (GAAP), employer demand for financial reporting KSAs will change quantitatively and qualitatively as the process of Convergence continues.

The reasons for the coming changes in the demand for financial reporting KSAs in U.S. labor markets include:

- Public companies in the United States will eventually be required to
  adopt the future set of country-neutral financial reporting standards
  that U.S. GAAP and International Financial Reporting Standards (IFRS)
  are converging into. That set of standards will be very different from
  current U.S. GAAP.
- Prior to the required adoption of future converged standards, some
  public companies in the United States will elect to adopt current IFRS
  for a variety of reasons (e.g., the desire to simplify the preparation of
  consolidated financial statements when a reporting entity is the parent
  of subsidiaries in multiple countries). Current IFRS differ significantly
  from current U.S. GAAP.
- Private companies in the United States have already begun to adopt
  current IFRS for a variety of reasons. In some cases, those companies
  are owned by foreign parents that have adopted IFRS. In other cases,
  private companies want to facilitate the raising of capital outside of the
  United States or to make themselves more attractive to potential foreign
  acquirers.
- All private companies in the United States will eventually switch to
  financial reporting standards other than current U.S. GAAP, although
  it is not clear at this time what private companies will switch to (see
  Chapter 6).
- There is a growing need for U.S. companies to be able to analyze
  IFRS financial statements during due diligence of foreign acquisition
  candidates.

For these reasons and others, Convergence will change the demand
for financial reporting KSAs in U.S. labor markets and thus obsolesce the
existing KSAs of workers who participate in those markets.

Quantitative Changes in Demand

One of the ways in which Convergence will change employer demand
for financial reporting talent in U.S. labor markets is that Convergence will
eliminate some of kinds of financial reporting work that must now be done.
Certain kinds of work that must be done in a world of many country-specific
sets of financial reporting standards will not need to be done in a world
that has embraced a single set of country-neutral standards. For example,
U.S. companies that are the parents of foreign subsidiaries would no longer

have to translate subsidiaries' financial statements into U.S. GAAP prior to preparing consolidated financial statements if both the parent and subsidiary were to use a single set of country-neutral financial reporting standards.

By permanently eliminating employers' demand for certain kinds of financial reporting work, the shift toward globally converged standards will quantitatively reduce the overall demand for financial reporting talent. This represents what economists call a *structural change* in the demand for labor, and could result in a certain degree of *structural unemployment* among workers who participate in U.S. labor markets for financial reporting talent.

In addition to causing quantitative structural changes in employers' demand for financial reporting talent, Convergence will also cause qualitative structural changes in demand. But the effects of the two kinds of structural changes will be very different in scope. Whereas the quantitative changes in demand will affect only a relatively small number of workers who participate in U.S. labor markets for financial reporting talent, the qualitative changes will affect almost all workers in those markets.

Qualitative Changes in Demand

In the United States and throughout the world, most kinds of financial reporting work that must be done today will still need to be done going forward. However, as a result of Convergence, future financial reporting work will need to be done in accordance with significantly different financial reporting standards. Thus, employers' demand for financial reporting talent can be expected to change qualitatively as a result of Convergence.

Specifically in the United States, nearly all financial reporting work is currently done in accordance with U.S. GAAP. As Convergence changes U.S. GAAP, U.S. employers' demand for financial reporting KSAs will change qualitatively. The impact on workers will be pervasive, as nearly all workers who participate in U.S. labor markets for financial reporting talent possess KSAs that will be rendered obsolete by qualitative changes in employers' demand.

Certain characteristics of U.S. GAAP have had a particularly strong influence on the financial reporting KSAs that are now bought and sold in U.S. labor markets. Therefore, the impact of Convergence on those characteristics will result in disproportionately significant qualitative changes to employer demand for financial reporting KSAs in U.S. labor markets. In particular, financial reporting KSAs in U.S. labor markets are what they are to a large extent because U.S. GAAP is voluminous,[1] poorly organized,[2] and substantively complex.[3] Because future converged standards are likely to exhibit those characteristics to a far lesser degree than current U.S. GAAP does, future financial reporting KSAs demanded by employers in U.S. labor markets are likely to differ significantly from the KSAs that employers currently demand.

Perhaps the most significant qualitative change in that regard will result from the efforts of the Financial Accounting Standards Board (FASB) and International Accounting Standards Board (IASB) to make future converged standards less rules based than U.S. GAAP is today (see Chapter 5). If the boards succeed, U.S. workers will find that employers will expect them to possess the KSAs needed to exercise professional judgment to a greater degree than current U.S. GAAP requires or allows.

Short-Term Imbalances in Supply and Demand

As employer demand for financial reporting KSAs changes quantitatively and qualitatively due to Convergence, changes in supply are unlikely to keep pace with changes in demand within U.S. labor markets for financial reporting talent. This is due to the relative inflexibility of the financial reporting talent "pipeline" in the United States (see Chapter 18).

Although any imbalances between supply and demand in U.S. labor markets for financial reporting talent are likely to be relatively short lived, they could still have a very significant impact. Even a relatively small shift in demand toward KSAs based on current IFRS would have the potential to redistribute career opportunities and earning power among individual workers in a manner similar to the impact of the Sarbanes-Oxley Act of 2002. The minority of workers who possess the newly demanded KSAs will be able to "write their own ticket," whereas workers who lack those KSAs will find themselves competing for the decreasing number of jobs in which the new KSAs are not needed.

Conclusion

Workers who participate in U.S. labor markets for financial reporting talent will be challenged to acquire new KSAs as Convergence renders existing KSAs based on current U.S. GAAP obsolete. You will find guidance on handling the managerial and personal challenges associated with the obsolescence of financial reporting KSAs in Chapters 21 and 22. But there are still several additional aspects of the impact of Convergence on U.S. labor markets that you should be aware of, such as the commoditization of financial reporting talent, which is examined in the next chapter.

Notes

1. See Glenn Cheney, "FASB Poised to Release GAAP Codification," *Accounting Today*, November 26, 2007.
2. Note that the FASB *Accounting Standards Codification* is slated to significantly improve the organization of U.S. GAAP.
3. See SEC Advisory Committee on Improvements to Financial Reporting, *Final Report of the Advisory Committee on Improvements to Financial Reporting to the United States Securities and Exchange Commission,* August 1, 2008.

CHAPTER 16

Commoditization of Talent

This chapter will explain the commoditization of financial reporting talent, the second of the four significant effects that Convergence will have on U.S. labor markets.

Global Homogenization of Employers' Demand

To understand the phenomenon of commoditization, it is helpful to recall three key points from prior chapters:

1. U.S. labor markets for financial reporting talent are based on knowledge, skills, and abilities (KSAs) that have traditionally differed from the KSAs bought and sold in other countries' labor markets for financial reporting talent (see Chapter 14).
2. The financial reporting KSAs demanded by U.S. employers will change as Convergence changes the financial reporting standards that those employers use (see Chapter 15).
3. Convergence is eliminating differences between the financial reporting standards used by U.S. employers and the standards used by employers in other countries (see Chapter 1).

Consequently, as employers in the United States and around the world come to use financial reporting standards that differ less and less among countries over time, the financial reporting KSAs demanded of workers will also differ less and less throughout the world's labor markets. Ultimately, sameness in financial reporting standards among countries will lead to sameness in the financial reporting KSAs that are bought and sold in the world's labor markets. And so, beyond simply changing employers' demand for financial reporting KSAs within individual labor markets, Convergence is homogenizing employers' demand for financial reporting KSAs across all labor markets.

With the widespread adoption of current International Financial Reporting Standards (IFRS) by more than 112 countries, global homogenization of employer demand for financial reporting KSAs is already well under way and can be expected to accelerate in the short term as a result of continued Convergence.

From Demand Homogenization to Supply Commoditization

As Convergence causes employers' demand for financial reporting KSAs to change both quantitatively and qualitatively in individual labor markets, workers in each market face the choice of either adapting to the changes in employers' demand or exiting the market. Workers who choose to adapt their financial reporting KSAs to the changing demand of employers will find themselves acquiring the same KSAs that workers throughout the rest of the world are acquiring due to the global homogenization of employer demand.

Thus, the global homogenization of demand for financial reporting KSAs is causing workers who represent the supply of financial reporting talent in the world's labor markets to become decreasingly distinct and increasingly interchangeable. An economist observing that phenomenon would say that the world's supply of financial reporting talent is becoming *commoditized*. To economists, a commodity is an undifferentiated product that is available from multiple producers. In other words, a commodity is a product that is essentially the same regardless of who produces it.

In past usage the term *commodity* has applied mainly to tangible goods, but in today's economy the term also applies to many intangible goods and services. Examples of tangible commodities include jet fuel and 24-karat gold. Examples of service commodities include the annual automobile inspections that most states require and commercial trash hauling.

In a very real sense, financial reporting talent is becoming a global commodity as a result of Convergence. Specifically, the global commoditization of financial reporting talent has already begun to occur as a result of workers' responses to the global homogenization of employers' demand for financial reporting KSAs. Soon, accountants in India will possess the same set of technical KSAs as accountants in Indiana. But will commoditization change employers' sourcing practices for financial reporting talent? Increasingly, the answer to that question is "yes"—employers will have both opportunities and incentives to source financial reporting talent globally instead of locally.

Intermarket Mobility of Employers

As explained in Chapter 14, a major reason that U.S. labor markets for financial reporting talent have largely been isolated from other countries' labor markets is that U.S. employers have traditionally demanded country-specific financial reporting KSAs from workers, and U.S. workers have supplied those KSAs on a nearly exclusive basis. Consequently, U.S. employers have had little incentive to participate in the labor markets for financial reporting talent that non-U.S. workers participate in. But the global commoditization of financial reporting talent is causing employers' behavior in labor markets to change.

As financial reporting talent becomes a global commodity in response to the global homogenization of employer demand, individual employers throughout the world are recognizing that they are no longer confined to country-specific labor markets by country-specific KSAs. This emerging opportunity for employers to participate in multiple countries' labor markets for financial reporting talent has been accompanied by the incentive to do so as a result of the specific manner in which financial reporting talent is becoming a global commodity. Because of this new opportunity and incentive, employers have begun to expand the geographic scope of their talent-sourcing practices from local to global.

Convergence-related changes in employer demand for financial reporting KSAs have occurred in some labor markets sooner than in others. Responsive changes in the supply of financial reporting talent have therefore occurred in some labor markets sooner than in others. Consequently, some labor markets currently have a significantly greater supply of commoditized financial reporting talent than others. But in nearly every labor market, the supply of financial reporting talent has responded relatively slowly to changes in employer demand, as noted in Chapter 15. Thus, the demand for commoditized financial reporting talent currently exceeds the available supply in most markets.

In the short term, the relative scarcity and nonuniform availability of commoditized financial reporting talent among the world's labor markets provides a strong incentive for employers to participate in labor markets other than their traditional ones. That is, employers now have an incentive to exhibit *intermarket mobility* among labor markets for financial reporting talent. That incentive is the direct result of supply lagging demand in all labor markets and the supply in some labor markets being greater than the supply in other labor markets. Specifically, employers in labor markets having a lesser supply of commoditized financial reporting talent have begun to enter labor markets having a greater supply of commoditized financial reporting talent.

An analogy may help explain the more abstract aspects of intermarket mobility. Say you have invited many guests to a cookout at your home. But on the day of the event, you realize that you have no propane for your new outdoor grill, which you recently purchased as a replacement for your old charcoal grill. If you drive to the local convenience store where you used to buy charcoal and find that the store does not sell propane, you will probably alter your "grill-fuel sourcing practices" rather than simply going home and canceling the cookout. Specifically, you will probably drive around to different stores to see if they sell propane, even in parts of town where you do not normally shop, until you find a store that does. Fortunately, it does not matter where you get the propane as long as you get it, because propane is a commodity. And even though it may cost more in time and effort to get the propane than it used to take you to get charcoal, you will still be able to hold your cookout as scheduled despite the qualitative change in your demand for grill fuel.

In the preceding example, you are likely to instinctively engage in intermarket mobility in order to obtain a commodity for which you have an immediate need but that is not available in your usual local market. Employers are now doing the same thing with regard to financial reporting talent. They find themselves with new needs for a commodity that they have not traditionally needed. When they find that the needed commodity is unavailable or scarce in their usual local labor markets, they instinctively look in other markets where the commodity is known to be available.

Of course, in the propane example, there were no prohibitive barriers to intermarket mobility—just a little extra time and effort on your part. But as described in Chapter 14, effective barriers to employer and worker mobility among different countries' labor markets often exist in the real world. If those barriers remain in place, intermarket mobility of employers will remain constrained.

Those barriers, however, are actually disappearing for reasons completely independent of Convergence. And the disappearance of long-standing legal, physical, and other barriers to employers' intermarket mobility, combined with the effects of the global commoditization of financial reporting talent, will have a profound impact on workers in U.S. labor markets, as explained in Chapter 17.

Conclusion

As a result of eliminating differences in financial reporting standards among countries, Convergence is homogenizing employer demand for financial reporting talent on a global scale. That homogenization is, in turn, causing the commoditization of financial reporting talent on a global scale. And in the short term, the differential rates of commoditization among the world's labor markets for financial reporting talent are causing employers to increasingly "think globally" when sourcing talent. Longer term, in conjunction with the factors discussed in Chapter 17, commoditization will have an even more profound impact on the world's labor markets for financial reporting talent.

CHAPTER 17

Toward a Global Labor Market for Financial Reporting Talent

As explained in Chapter 16, employers' demand for financial reporting knowledge, skills, and abilities (KSAs) is becoming increasingly homogeneous throughout the world as a result of Convergence. In response, the supply of financial reporting talent is becoming increasingly commoditized on a global scale. The homogenization of demand and the commoditization of supply have in turn led to an increase in the mobility of employers among multiple labor markets for financial reporting talent. But even so, the world's labor markets for financial reporting talent have remained largely segregated from each other due to the existence of linguistic, cultural, legal, and physical constraints on the geographic scope of those markets.

If the traditional constraints on the geographic scope of labor markets for financial reporting talent were to persist, the high degree of segregation among those markets would persist as well. But the constraints have started to disappear, and because they are disappearing, Convergence has begun to have an additional impact on labor markets that it has not previously had. That impact represents the third of the four significant effects that Convergence is having on labor markets in general and U.S. labor markets in particular.

This chapter will explain the unique way in which labor markets for financial reporting talent in the United States and throughout the world are changing specifically as a result of the combination of Convergence and the disappearance of constraints on the markets' geographic scope. This chapter will also discuss the profound implications for employers and workers who participate in U.S. labor markets for financial reporting talent.

177

Global Desegregation of Labor Markets

Recall from Chapter 14 that the world's numerous labor markets for financial reporting talent have traditionally been narrow in geographic scope and highly segregated from each other for many reasons. One by one, however, those reasons are fading away due to Convergence and other trends. The overall effect is that labor markets for financial reporting talent are desegregating globally. This section will explain the trends behind the global desegregation of labor markets for financial reporting talent.

Role of Convergence

In the past, a primary reason for the segregation of labor markets for financial reporting talent was that such markets were based on KSAs that differed significantly among countries. While market segregation has historically been reinforced by other factors, country-specific differences among financial reporting KSAs would result in a high degree of labor-market segregation even in the absence of reinforcing factors.

Of course, Convergence is eliminating country-specific differences in the financial reporting KSAs that are bought and sold in different labor markets throughout the world. By itself, the elimination of differences among the financial reporting KSAs on which different labor markets are based cannot be expected to result in labor-market desegregation. But it represents the removal a key obstacle, allowing desegregation to occur as other constraints disappear. And those other constraints are indeed disappearing.

Role of Technology

Another primary cause of segregation among labor markets for financial reporting talent has been the existence of physical, legal, and cultural constraints on the markets' geographic scope. Historically, those constraints have reinforced KSA-based market segregation, but they have also proven themselves to be capable of maintaining a high degree of market segregation even as the demand for financial reporting KSAs homogenizes and the supply commoditizes worldwide. However, such constraints on the geographic scope of labor markets have begun to disappear, for reasons largely unrelated to Convergence.

Specifically, advances in technology are responsible for eliminating physical constraints on the geographic scope of labor markets for financial reporting talent. Advances in telecommunications and computing technology in particular have made it possible for employers and workers to overcome many of the physical constraints that previously made it necessary for workers to assemble in person at a particular location. Even though employers' preferences for having workers physically present have been slow to change in response to technological advances, "telework" is becoming increasingly acceptable to employers, at least some of the time for at least some of the workforce.

The elimination of constraints on the physical location of workers has made it possible to overcome legal constraints as well. Companies employing teleworkers have been created outside of the United States specifically for the purpose of selling workers' labor to U.S. employers on a contractual basis, thus effectively circumventing the constraints of national labor laws regarding whom an employer may employ. In some cases, U.S. employers have set up such companies on a captive basis, again without having to worry about immigration or related employment barriers. As most corporate financial managers know, "offshoring" is already a common and rapidly growing practice, particularly in the field of accounting and financial reporting.[1]

Cultural constraints on the geographic scope of labor markets are also fading as a result of technology. In particular, the Internet provides billions of people throughout the world with opportunities to be exposed to cultures other than their own and to engage in interpersonal social communication on a scale that was unimaginable only a generation ago. Although the Internet is not quite transforming the world into one big melting pot, people in foreign countries are not so foreign to Americans anymore, and vice versa.

Other Factors

There are several additional factors that are contributing to the global desegregation of the world's labor markets for financial reporting talent. One is the globally pervasive use of the English language in accounting and finance.

It has long been said that accounting is the language of business. Today, a valid corollary to that statement is that English is the language of accounting—worldwide. While in the past, language has served to segregate labor markets for financial reporting talent, now language—specifically the English language—is helping to unite those markets. Financial professionals around the world whose primary language is not English are learning English in large numbers. A global certification has even been developed to attest to an individual's proficiency in "financial English."[2]

Another factor that is contributing to the desegregation of labor markets within the United States is that certified public accountants (CPAs) are enjoying greater interstate mobility as a result of the ongoing efforts of the American Institute of CPAs (AICPA) and the National Association of State Boards of Accountancy (NASBA). Additionally, reciprocal recognition of credentials similar to the CPA credential is becoming more commonplace among countries.

Finally, the globalization of capital markets in particular and business in general is exerting pressure on labor markets for financial reporting talent to desegregate.

Synergy among Factors

It is important to recognize that no one of the above factors by itself could drive market desegregation. But together the factors are bringing overwhelming change to the world's labor markets for financial reporting talent. Specifically, all of the factors in combination with each other are causing the supply of and demand for financial reporting talent to become increasingly global in scope. As a result, the numerous labor markets for financial reporting talent around the world are desegregating into far fewer markets, each having geographic scope that extends far beyond any individual country. Desegregation also carries profound implications for employers and workers who participate in labor markets for financial reporting talent, as discussed in the next section.

Competition in the Global Labor Market

When segregated commodity markets desegregate, economic theory predicts that the level of competitiveness in the combined market will be greater than the level of competitiveness in the separate markets. More than just the psychological state of market participants, *competitiveness* refers to specific economic characteristics that a market may or may not exhibit. This section will explain the impact of the global desegregation of labor markets for financial reporting talent on the competitiveness of the markets themselves and on employers and workers who participate in those markets.

How Desegregation Will Make Labor Markets More Competitive

Economists consider a market to be "perfectly competitive" if it exhibits certain characteristics. For example, for a market to be perfectly competitive, the product or service that is bought and sold in the market must be a commodity (i.e., identical regardless of who buys or sells it). There must also be a large number of buyers and sellers in the market such that no one buyer or seller can influence the prevailing price in the market.

Although perfectly competitive markets do not exist in the real world, some markets exhibit the characteristics of perfect competition to a much greater degree than others. The more a market exhibits the characteristics of perfect competition, the more competitive the market is said to be. Thus, a single market consisting of a certain number of buyers and sellers is inherently more competitive than if the same total number of buyers and sellers were to be separated into several smaller markets. And the more similar a market's products or services are to each other, the more competitive the market. Consequently, as the supply of financial reporting talent commoditizes and labor markets for financial reporting talent desegregate, we will end up with far fewer—but far more competitive—markets.

Why Market Competitiveness Matters to Market Participants

From a buyer's perspective, increased competition in a market is a good thing. It enables buyers to obtain what they seek from a larger pool of sellers, making buyers less dependent on particular sellers and less likely to be adversely impacted by the exit of an individual seller from the market. From a seller's perspective, however, increased competition in a market is not so good. While it makes sellers less dependent on particular buyers, it also brings more sellers into direct competition with each other.

In competitive markets, sellers find themselves in the position of being *price takers*—they cannot individually dictate prices, they can only accept the prices set by aggregate forces of the market. The prevailing price in a competitive market is quickly established at the lowest level that will keep just enough sellers in the market to satisfy demand at that price. Any seller who attempts to charge a higher price than other sellers will not succeed in selling because even if a buyer is willing to buy at that price, that buyer could easily find a seller who is willing to sell at a lower price. And any seller who attempts to charge a lower price than other sellers is foolish, as that seller could easily find a buyer who is willing to pay a higher price. Thus, with strong disincentives to charge prices other than those determined by aggregate market forces, prices in commodity markets are far more uniform than they would be if the products in the market were qualitatively different from each other. And prices in more competitive markets tend to be far lower than they would be in less competitive markets.

Employers, as buyers of financial reporting talent in labor markets, welcome the increased competitiveness that the commoditization of financial reporting talent and the desegregation of labor markets will bring. In particular, employers desire the lower wages that they would be able to pay in more competitive labor markets. However, workers, as sellers of labor, will be adversely affected by an increase in the competitiveness of the market in which they participate, since increased competitiveness will be accompanied by lower wage levels and a reduction in bargaining power.

The long-term prospects for U.S. workers and employers are very clear: As the world's employers find themselves facing a global pool of talent in which all workers have the same KSAs needed to do the financial reporting work that needs to be done everywhere in the world—and who can do the work from India just as easily as from Indiana—then financial reporting work will go to workers who are willing to accept the lowest wages. Consequently, "U.S. accountants could find themselves to be small fish in a big global pool of accountants—all of whom will be qualified to compete against each other for jobs anywhere in the world, and most of whom will be willing to work for far less compensation than U.S. accountants now enjoy."[3]

Example from Recent History

Not everyone is willing to accept the long-term inevitability of a highly competitive, global labor market for financial reporting talent. But skeptics may wish to note the parallels that exist between present and emerging factors in labor markets for financial reporting talent and factors that were present in other labor markets that have undergone profound change.

For example, U.S. labor markets for information technology (IT) design and development talent underwent a profound transformation in the early years of the twenty-first century. Up to that time, U.S. employers and U.S. IT workers participated in labor markets that were largely country specific and segregated from the world's other labor markets for IT talent. Within a brief period, however, U.S. employers dramatically shifted their employment practices and began to rely far more heavily on offshore IT workers than on U.S. workers. Prevailing wage levels plummeted from the levels that previously existed in U.S. markets. Many U.S. IT professionals found themselves unemployed or underemployed.

What led to that shift? Essentially the same factors that are present and emerging in U.S. labor markets for financial reporting talent:

- Technical KSAs that are country neutral, globally demanded, and largely commoditized
- The amenability of the work to being done remotely with the aid of technology
- The ability and willingness of employers and workers to transcend national or ethnic cultural differences
- Pervasive use of the English language
- Portable certifications of technical KSAs

Not all U.S. employers in the globalized market for IT talent have been satisfied with the quality of the talent they have purchased abroad. But few employers are able to resist the economic lure of lower costs at least on an experimental basis. What happened to U.S. labor markets for IT talent could easily happen again to U.S. labor markets for financial reporting talent.[4]

Conclusion

Time and time again, U.S. workers have seen their foreign counterparts gain the capacity and opportunity to provide the KSAs that U.S. employers demand at lower wages. As a result of Convergence and other trends, that phenomenon now threatens to occur in U.S. labor markets for financial reporting talent.

Also as a result of Convergence and other trends, labor markets for financial reporting talent become fewer in number, global in geographic scope, and far more competitive. Additionally, employers have significant economic incentive to facilitate market desegregation. The long-term result will be that financial reporting workers in the United States and around the world will be in direct competition with each other. Employers will clearly benefit from that situation, but workers will not, especially workers who are accustomed to high wages and who are slow to respond to changes in employer demand for financial reporting KSAs.

Notes

1. Alan Rappeport, "Offshoring Is Still Going Strong," August 14, 2008, available at www.cfo.com/article.cfm/11949318.
2. See www.FinancialEnglish.org for a description of the "International Certificate in Financial English" offered jointly by the University of Cambridge and the Association of Chartered Certified Accountants.
3. AccountingWEB, Inc., "A Conversation with Bruce Pounder: Accountants Cannot Ignore Convergence," June 15, 2007, available at www.accountingweb.com/cgi-bin/item.cgi?id=103630.
4. See SmartPros, "Offshoring Threatens U.S. Accountants, Says Economist," May 14, 2007, available at http://accounting.smartpros.com/x57660.xml.

CHAPTER 18

Transformation of the Talent Supply Pipeline

As noted in previous chapters, employers' demand for financial reporting talent in U.S. labor markets is changing quantitatively and qualitatively as a result of Convergence. Changes in employers' demand for financial reporting talent are driving changes in the supply of that talent. And changes in both the demand for and supply of financial reporting talent are causing labor markets themselves to change in the United States and throughout the world.

This chapter looks beyond the interaction of supply and demand in U.S. labor markets to examine the impact of Convergence on the "pipeline" that supplies financial reporting talent to those markets. That impact represents the last of the four significant effects of Convergence examined in Part Three.

Overview of the U.S. Talent Supply Pipeline

Each of the world's labor markets for financial reporting talent is dependent on individuals, institutions, and activities that collectively constitute a "pipeline" that supplies talent to the market. The characteristics of a labor market's supply pipeline ultimately determine the quantity and quality of talent available to employers. Traditionally, the various components of most markets' pipelines have been country specific in nature, although like labor markets themselves, some components have had a narrower geographic focus.

Because workers who participate in labor markets for financial reporting talent are expected to possess relatively high levels of knowledge, skills, and abilities (KSAs), education is the primary function performed by pipelines that supply labor markets with financial reporting talent. A secondary function that financial reporting talent pipelines perform is certification of individual workers' KSAs.

In the United States, as in most countries, nearly every aspect of the financial reporting talent pipeline is predicated on a high degree of quantitative and qualitative stability in the demand for the KSAs that are bought and sold in labor markets. This characteristic makes for a pipeline that lacks the agility to anticipate or react to changes in market demand for financial reporting KSAs. That lack of agility in turn represents a risk that the U.S. talent supply pipeline may not be sustainable in the long run if more agile pipelines elsewhere in the world demonstrate superior relevance to the emerging global labor market for financial reporting talent.

Educational Activities in the U.S. Talent Supply Pipeline

The educational activities that occur within the U.S. supply pipeline for financial reporting talent fall into three categories:

1. Formal preparatory education
2. On-the-job education
3. Formal continuing education

Because the KSAs that are bought and sold in U.S. labor markets for financial reporting talent have traditionally been based on U.S. generally accepted accounting principles (GAAP), so have the educational activities of the talent pipeline that supplies U.S. labor markets. Although Convergence has already begun to obsolesce the GAAP-based KSAs that have traditionally been demanded in U.S. labor markets, the U.S. pipeline's educational activities remain firmly focused on U.S. GAAP. However, the overall scope of the pipeline's educational activities has broadened to include the commoditized, country-neutral KSAs that employers increasingly demand. And the level of educational activity in the pipeline has started to intensify, as working professionals engage in additional learning activities to acquire new KSAs, whether out of opportunity or necessity.

Formal Preparatory Education

In the United States, formal preparatory education for a professional career in financial accounting and reporting is a multiyear process that takes place in colleges and universities. As such, the preparatory education of professional-level accounting and finance workers is shaped in part by the distinctive characteristics of the U.S. postsecondary education system. That system differs from the postsecondary education systems of other countries in many ways, including overall educational objectives, relative affordability, selectivity of admissions, and duration of study programs. Those characteristics also vary considerably among institutions of higher learning within the United States.

Preparatory education for U.S. accounting and finance professionals is also shaped by another significant factor. Degree programs in accounting at U.S. colleges and universities are heavily geared toward producing graduates who are qualified to work in entry-level jobs at public accounting firms, especially firms that serve primarily as external auditors of business entities. That situation has been perpetuated through the substantial financial and technical support of college accounting programs by public accounting firms themselves, especially the larger firms.

The business models of many public accounting firms are predicated on access to a steady stream of relatively skilled yet relatively low-cost workers coming out of U.S. colleges and universities, and consequently such firms are the foremost employers of graduates holding degrees in accounting. While heads of college accounting departments bitterly deny the vocational nature of the education that they provide to students, those departments would cease to exist in the absence of the symbiotic relationship that they have with the major employers of their graduates.

Thus, the talent needs of public accounting firms effectively dictate the KSAs with which U.S. college accounting programs imbue their graduates. At this time, those talent needs and their underlying KSAs are still based on U.S. GAAP because most firms' clients still require auditing and other services that are based on U.S. GAAP. But as Convergence alters the KSAs that public accounting firms demand from entry-level professionals, college accounting programs will have to change in response.

The problem is that college accounting programs are unable to change quickly in response to changes in the KSAs that graduates are expected to possess. Faculty competencies, textbooks, and degree curricula each take years to change. Consequently, the only realistic hope that public accounting firms have of avoiding shortages of qualified entry-level talent in the future is to initiate and support changes in college accounting programs in the present. And the largest public accounting firms have begun to do just that, through recently launched programs that provide technical and financial support for proactive change in U.S. college accounting programs.[1] Without that support and its implicit signaling of employers' future KSA needs, college accounting programs would have neither the resources nor incentive to change on their own.

Despite the support they are receiving from public accounting firms, U.S. accounting educators should recognize that Convergence will still impose challenges on them. For example, Convergence-induced changes in college accounting programs are coming at a time when there is a widespread shortage of academically qualified accounting professors in the United States. U.S. colleges and universities are therefore likely to find themselves shorthanded when implementing the changes that must be made to their accounting programs.

Pedagogical challenges also await educators. For example, as financial accounting and reporting in the United States becomes less about "following the rules" and more about exercising professional judgment, educators will certainly find it more challenging to teach professional judgment to accounting students than to teach those students how to follow rules.

It is also important to recognize that while Convergence will compel U.S. colleges and universities to teach future global financial reporting standards in the long term, getting U.S. colleges and universities to teach current International Financial Reporting Standards (IFRS) in the short term is *not* on the critical path to Convergence. What is far more critical in the short term is addressing the retraining of working professionals through on-the-job and formal continuing education. The challenges associated with doing so differ substantially from the challenges associated with overhauling the formal preparatory education of accounting and finance workers.

On-the-Job Education

In the United States, as in most parts of the world, a significant portion of accounting and finance workers' professional education has traditionally occurred on the job. However, the on-the-job educational opportunities that an individual worker is exposed to are entirely dependent on the business needs and employee-development practices of that individual's current employer. Such business needs and practices may be highly unrepresentative of those of other employers in the financial reporting supply chain. Also, some employers are much slower than other employers to adapt to externally imposed change. So unless individual U.S. employers anticipate and respond to Convergence in an appropriate way, the accounting and finance workers that they employ are at risk of being left behind in terms of acquiring the KSAs they will need to succeed in a world of converged financial reporting standards.

In large companies, in-house KSA-development programs, "centers of excellence," and "communities of practice" have often been implemented successfully to provide on-the-job education in connection with large-scale change initiatives. Such techniques may work for Convergence as well, and are likely to be the most effective ways to help workers develop sound professional judgment. But those techniques are simply not feasible for smaller companies, which will be forced to rely more on outside talent, outside coaching, and "study groups" banding together across companies. In particular, the "OFO" (*only* financial officer) has little hope of teaching himself essential KSAs while doing his regular job and doing all the extra tasks that Convergence will require.[2] Thus, in the near future, on-the-job education will probably be a less prominent component of the educational activities that occur in the U.S. pipeline for financial reporting talent than it is today, especially for smaller U.S. companies. And formal continuing education is likely to rise in prominence in order to compensate for the limitations of on-the-job education.

Formal Continuing Education

Formal continuing education for accounting and finance professionals is already a big business in the United States. A large part of the demand for such education comes from the continuing professional education (CPE) requirements that hundreds of thousands of U.S. certified public accountants (CPAs) are subject to as a condition of maintaining licensure and/or membership in professional associations. Other certified professionals, such as certified management accountants (CMAs) and certified internal auditors (CIAs), are subject to similar requirements.

On the supply side, the market for continuing education in accounting and finance is dominated by large professional associations such as the American Institute of CPAs (AICPA) and state CPA societies. In addition to those organizations, there are thousands of small, independent education providers who also supply the market.

In today's market for continuing education in accounting and finance, supply is poorly aligned with demand on the key dimension of *relevance*. One reason for the mismatch is that the business models of the biggest providers are based on a lengthy development-to-delivery cycle that in some cases exceeds two years. Because major developments in Convergence and other areas of accounting and finance occur on a weekly basis, the dominant providers in the market have not been able to get relevant content to market before it becomes obsolete. Certain smaller independent providers have used this to their competitive advantage, as those providers tend to be more agile and have therefore been able to supply highly relevant educational content to the market thanks to a development-to-delivery cycle that is better measured in hours rather than months.

Retraining the one-million-plus working professionals in the U.S. talent pipeline—essentially all at once—will be the challenge that continuing education providers must prepare themselves to meet as a matter of their own survival as well as the global competitiveness of the U.S. supply pipeline for financial reporting talent. The large professional associations, having the most to lose as a result of being incapable of meeting demand for Convergence-related continuing education and having few prospects of becoming more agile in the short term, will have little choice but to partner with more-agile independent CPE providers. And the independent CPE providers will benefit from the effective large-scale marketing efforts of the associations. Fortunately, professional associations and independent CPE providers have already begun to form these types of partnerships.

Certification of KSAs

As noted earlier in this chapter, a secondary function that the U.S. financial reporting talent supply pipeline performs is certification of individual workers' KSAs. Certification is usually dependent on an individual's satisfying specific education, examination, and experience requirements. In the United States, the most well-known example of KSA certification in financial accounting and reporting is the CPA credential. However, there are many other certifications for accounting and finance professionals, such as the CMA and CIA credentials.

The CPA, CMA, and other credentials differ from each other in terms of the set of KSAs that each credential attests to. In that regard, the relevance of specific credentials to U.S. labor markets has begun to change as a result of Convergence. Currently, most of the credentials commonly found in the United States attest to KSAs that are based on current U.S. GAAP. But credentials based on current IFRS, such as the Diploma in International Financial Reporting (DipIFR) awarded by the Association of Chartered Certified Accountants, are gaining in prominence.

There are also significant differences in geographic scope among credentials. For example, in the United States, the CPA credential is granted at the state level and consequently has restricted interstate and international portability.[3] In contrast, the CMA and DipIFR credentials are global in scope and thus universally portable. The significance of the geographic scope of a particular credential should be obvious by now: in a time of global markets for goods and services, global markets for capital, and global markets for financial reporting talent, as well as global financial reporting standards, accounting and finance credentials that are not globally portable do not appear to be sustainable.[4]

Despite the differences among accounting and finance credentials, credentialing organizations face a common challenge: the KSAs that their credentials currently attest to are becoming obsolete as a result of Convergence. And the lead time required to reflect necessary changes in the credentialing examinations, such as the U.S. Uniform CPA Examination, is very long, often a matter of years.[5] Thus, in the area of certification, as in education, a lack of agility again threatens the global competitiveness of the U.S. supply pipeline for financial reporting talent.

Interpipeline Competition

As explained earlier in this chapter, the educational and certification functions of the U.S. supply pipeline for financial reporting talent suffer from a significant lack of agility. The lack of agility in those functions creates the risk that the U.S. pipeline as a whole may become irrelevant to the increasingly globalized labor markets for financial reporting talent, because there are many similar pipelines around the world that exhibit greater agility.

A lack of agility is not the only threat to the global competitiveness of the U.S. talent pipeline. Developing countries such as India and China have the potential to add to the world's supply of accounting and finance professionals on a scale and at a rate that far exceed the capabilities of the United States and other developed countries. If developing countries choose to do so, they can rapidly and significantly increase the number of workers who possess the commoditized financial reporting KSAs that employers around the world increasingly demand.

As long as their domestic labor markets remained segregated from other countries' labor markets, developing countries have not needed or wanted to increase the capacity of their financial reporting talent pipelines. But as a result of the global desegregation of labor markets for financial reporting talent (see Chapter 17), developing countries have both the opportunity and incentive to scale up the capacity of their pipelines for financial reporting talent.

Flooding the global labor market with relatively low-cost talent could force much of the high-cost talent from the United States and other developed countries out of that market. And a collapse in the number of U.S. workers who are able to compete successfully in the future global labor market for financial reporting talent would render the U.S. talent supply pipeline largely obsolete. At that point, the U.S. pipeline would suffer from capacity far in excess of demand, and the result would be a major quantitative structural change in demand for the individuals, institutions, and information resources that make up the pipeline.

Conclusion

Not only is Convergence increasing the level of competition among individual workers who participate in the world's labor markets for financial reporting talent, Convergence is also increasing competition among the pipelines that supply financial reporting talent to labor markets. As a result, the U.S. talent supply pipeline will be challenged to transform itself in order to survive.

Notes

1. Roy Harris, "Big Four Make Big Plans for IFRS" [online], May 22, 2008, available at: www.cfo.com/article.cfm/11434822.
2. The term *Only Financial Officer* has been popularized by John L. Daly in the professional education courses that he teaches.
3. As noted in Chapter 17, the efforts of the American Institute of CPAs and the National Association of State Boards of Accountancy have begun to loosen such restrictions.
4. It is interesting to note that a multinational, multiyear attempt led by the AICPA to establish a global business credential came to an unsuccessful end in 2002. It remains to be seen if the passage of time will change sentiment toward such a credential.
5. As an example, in May 2008, the AICPA's Board of Examiners issued an exposure draft of proposed content and skill specifications for the Uniform CPA Examination. The proposed content specification outlines include, for the first time, IFRS-related topics in the Financial Accounting and Reporting section of the exam. The exposure draft was the result of approximately two years of work and, if approved, would not be implemented until approximately two years after approval.

Part III Epilogue

The key points of Part III can be summarized as follows:

1. Employers in the United States have a decreasing need for financial reporting KSAs that are based on current U.S. GAAP. (See Chapter 15.)
2. What U.S. employers need in terms of financial reporting talent increasingly resembles (1) what employers in other countries need and (2) what workers in other countries are increasingly able to supply. (See Chapter 16.)
3. U.S. employers now have a greater ability to obtain the financial reporting KSAs that they seek by sourcing financial reporting talent globally. (See Chapter 17.)
4. U.S. workers and the entire U.S. pipeline for financial reporting talent will either adapt to the above realities or become irrelevant. (See Chapter 18.)

The reason for all of the preceding is, of course, Convergence. Now that you have a better understanding of how Convergence is changing not only the technical aspects of financial reporting (as discussed in Part Two) but the livelihoods of financial reporting workers in the United States and throughout the world, you are ready for Part Four to guide you through the period of unprecedented change that Convergence has thrust us into.

PART IV

Preparing for the Impact of Convergence

Here, in Part Four, you will learn what to *do* about Convergence and *why* you should do it. Specifically, this part will:

- Explain the critical decisions and plans that you must make in order to prepare your company, department, and yourself for the growing impact of Convergence.
- Guide you in making and implementing your decisions and plans in order to prevent Convergence from interfering with the attainment of your company goals, department goals, and personal career goals.

More specifically, Chapter 19 will provide an overview of the three main challenges that Convergence will impose on corporate financial managers. The three subsequent chapters of Part Four will in turn help you prepare to overcome each of those challenges.

Your understanding of the material in Part Four will depend to a large extent on your understanding of everything that this book has covered so far. Part One described the phenomenon of Convergence, while Parts Two and Three explained the many direct and indirect effects that Convergence is having on financial reporting in the United States and on U.S. labor markets for financial reporting talent. If you skipped over any of those parts, consider going back now to at least skim through what you skipped; otherwise, you will not get the full benefit of this part.

CHAPTER 19

Overview of the Challenges of Convergence

From prior chapters, you now know that Convergence is directly affecting the financial reporting standards that U.S. companies use. You should also know that the indirect effects of Convergence extend far beyond changes in financial reporting standards. Given the nature, scope, and magnitude of the direct and indirect effects of Convergence, it should come as no surprise that professional success at an individual, department, or enterprise level will not happen if you simply leave everything to chance. Rather, your success will be determined by how well prepared you are for the impact of Convergence.

What corporate financial managers should do to prepare for the impact of Convergence is neither obvious nor simple. Therefore, you will need practical guidance. This chapter is the first of four chapters that will guide you in your preparation for the impact of Convergence. Specifically, it will provide you with an overview of the most significant managerial and personal challenges that you must recognize and overcome in order to succeed in this time of great change.

Why Preparation Matters

A fundamental premise of this book is that corporate financial managers are largely unprepared for the disruptive changes in the U.S. financial reporting environment that have begun to occur as a result of Convergence. There are several reasons why U.S. financial managers are not adequately prepared for the impact of Convergence, including:

- *A lack of awareness.* Many U.S. financial managers remain ignorant of the impact that Convergence will have on their jobs in the short term and on their careers in the long term.

- *Denial.* Some financial managers refuse to acknowledge the realities of Convergence due to its unwelcome implications.
- *Skepticism.* As a result of past experiences, managers may be reluctant to embrace any "next big thing" like Convergence. Often, a "next big thing" fails to live up to its hype, or is quickly overshadowed by something even bigger.
- *Overload.* In addition to Convergence, there are several other major developments affecting U.S. financial managers that seem to be coming all at the same time, such as XBRL and the Financial Accounting Standards Board's (FASB's) Accounting Standards Codification.
- *A lack of knowledge, skills, and abilities (KSAs).* The most pervasive cause of financial managers' lack of preparedness is that they simply do not possess the KSAs needed to deal effectively with the impact of Convergence. Fortunately, this is also the most actionable cause—by reading this book, for example, you can acquire KSAs that will markedly increase your level of preparedness for Convergence.

Although there are many different reasons why U.S. financial managers are unprepared or underprepared for the impact of Convergence, in every case the risk is the same: a lack of preparedness for Convergence is likely to be very costly for individuals, companies, and the U.S. economy as a whole.

One way to put the value of being prepared for Convergence into perspective is to compare Convergence to another recent source of significant change to the U.S. financial reporting environment: the Sarbanes-Oxley Act (SOX) of 2002. In the case of SOX, if financial managers had fully comprehended its impact before that impact occurred, many of them would have made very different managerial decisions for their companies and very different personal decisions for their careers. Different managerial decisions would have spared companies a lot of the costs and disruptions that accompanied SOX. And different personal decisions would have positioned individual managers to pursue and attain the highly desirable career opportunities that arose as a result of SOX.

With SOX, it was virtually impossible for anyone to accurately predict the nature, scope, and magnitude of its effects in advance. Fortunately, the effects of Convergence are much easier to foresee than the effects of SOX were. That means financial managers will be better able to prepare for the impact of Convergence than they were able to prepare for the impact of SOX. It is a good thing, too—Convergence will have a far greater impact than SOX has had.

Financial managers who take advantage of the opportunity to prepare for Convergence now are unlikely to look back ten years from now and wish they had made different decisions. And managers who distinguish themselves through superior preparedness for the impact of Convergence can expect to reap benefits for their employers, which will in turn translate into career benefits for the individual managers.

Three Challenges

Fundamentally, preparing for Convergence is about preparing for externally imposed change. Most people find it challenging to anticipate and respond to such change.

Of the many challenges associated with preparing for the impact of Convergence, three specific challenges stand out from the rest. The three challenges differ in scope, and will hereafter be referred to as:

- The enterprise challenge
- The departmental challenge
- The personal challenge

Preparing for the impact of Convergence will require financial managers to become intimately familiar with each of those challenges. But before examining them in detail, it is helpful to discuss a challenge that is not found among those top three. Specifically, "learning a different set of financial reporting standards" is not among the top challenges of Convergence. Even though you will certainly need to update your financial reporting KSAs as individual standards change and as companies change which set of standards they use, the technical challenge of doing so is actually rather minor compared to the managerial and personal challenges described below.

You should take encouragement from the fact that your experience as a financial professional will serve you well in dealing with the technical challenge of Convergence—possibly even better than you might have thought it would. But by the same token, you should not underestimate the managerial and personal challenges that await you—challenges that will require you to make certain decisions and plans and then act on them. It is those challenges that you should focus on preparing for now in order to have any hope of overcoming them.

Enterprise Challenge: Choosing Standards and Living with Your Choice

As explained in Chapter 1, two sets of standards currently dominate the world's corporate financial reporting landscape—U.S. generally accepted accounting principles (GAAP) and International Financial Reporting Standards (IFRS). Companies that do not use one of those sets of standards are unlikely to be able to compete successfully for the lowest-cost capital in the world's capital markets and may also be forced to obtain their financial reporting talent from uncompetitive labor markets.

Over the next ten years, Convergence will eliminate the differences between U.S. GAAP and IFRS such that a single set of converged financial reporting standards will be dominant worldwide. But until then, companies in the United States and throughout the world face the choice of whether to use U.S. GAAP or IFRS. And private companies have at least one additional option—the IFRS for Private Entities (see Chapter 6).

Consequently, the first major challenge of Convergence for a U.S. company—the enterprise-level challenge—is determining which set of financial reporting standards to use until Convergence has been achieved. In other words, each company must choose one of multiple paths toward a common future of converged financial reporting standards. The question of which path to take toward Convergence is not a trivial one, nor is the optimal choice as obvious as many U.S. financial managers think it is.

For U.S. public companies, the opportunity to choose to use a set of financial reporting standards other than U.S. GAAP was virtually unimaginable until only recently. And although U.S. private companies have long enjoyed the ability to choose their financial reporting standards, any private company bigger than a sole proprietorship has been almost certain to choose U.S. GAAP for practical reasons. Thus, the challenge of choosing a set of financial reporting standards is a new kind of challenge that most U.S. financial managers have never faced before. And today, managers face new incentives to think carefully about a choice that they may not have given any thought to in the past.

Each of the options that are available to companies will have different consequences, and the consequences of any given option may differ from company to company. In helping a company choose the financial reporting standards that are best for it to use, a financial manager must be prepared to analyze how a company's unique circumstances will subjectively shape the consequences associated with each option. And because a company's circumstances can change over time, financial managers must be prepared to reassess a company's choice of standards over time as circumstances change. Furthermore, regardless of the option that a company chooses, financial managers must be prepared to help their companies live with the consequences of their choices. Chapter 20 will help you prepare to lead your company to choose its financial reporting standards wisely and to live with its choice.

Departmental Challenge: Managing Talent

Closely related to the enterprise challenge, but narrower in scope, is the departmental challenge of managing talent. Regardless of a company's choice of financial reporting standards, Convergence will cause continuous change in the financial reporting KSAs that companies will require from workers.

Consequently, financial managers will be under continuous pressure to ensure that their existing staffs undergo necessary training and development. And as the nature of financial reporting standards migrates toward being less rules based, the nature of staff training and development may have to change as well.

Financial managers will also face increased pressure to identify, recruit, and retain workers who possess the KSAs needed by their companies. And in order for companies to remain competitive on a global basis, financial managers are likely to find themselves in new territory, literally and figuratively, as they are forced to expand the geographic scope of their talent management efforts beyond their traditional boundaries. In Chapter 21 you will find guidance on dealing with the talent management challenges that are resulting from Convergence.

Personal Challenge: Succeeding in a Hypercompetitive Labor Market

Whereas the first two major challenges of Convergence are managerial in nature, the third is personal in nature. Individual financial managers face a future of having to compete for jobs in global, hypercompetitive labor markets for financial reporting talent.

To adopt an effective mind-set toward preparing for the personal challenge of Convergence, begin by recognizing that the job you have today is not likely to be the job from which you will retire. And there are two things to keep in mind as you move closer to the last job of your career.

First, expect that the job you will retire from will be very different from the job you have today. In fact, it will be very different from the job that anyone you know has today. The day-to-day tasks will be substantially different as a direct result of Convergence.

Second, expect to encounter increasingly stiff competition to get and keep the job from which you will retire. The hypercompetitiveness of future labor markets, which will present substantial economic benefits to employers, will present substantial career challenges to you and your peers.

As further explained in Chapter 22, Convergence will challenge you to be *relevant*, *visible*, *distinct*, and *flexible* in order to succeed. These are not new keys to career success; they are just more difficult to attain because of Convergence. As a result, you may have to prepare to do things that you are not prepared to do today.

Conclusion

Each of the three main challenges—enterprise, department, and personal— is about coping effectively with externally imposed change in a dynamic business environment. Your success during this period of Convergence will depend at least as much on your planning and decision-making KSAs as on your technical KSAs.

Like any challenges, the three examined here in Part Four will be much less intimidating the better prepared you are for them. By reading this far, your preparation is off to a solid start. The remaining chapters of this part will build from here. Soon you will know what critical managerial and career plans and decisions you need to make, along with knowing how to make them in your unique circumstances, as Convergence continues to drive changes in financial reporting standards.

CHAPTER 20

The Enterprise Challenge: Strategies for Choosing Standards and Implementing Your Choice

As progress toward the goal of Convergence accelerates, public and private entities that report under U.S. generally accepted accounting principles (GAAP) are finding themselves with more opportunities to switch to International Financial Reporting Standards (IFRS). Remember, however, that having multiple sets of financial reporting standards for companies to choose from is fundamentally incompatible with the goal of Convergence. Thus, with regard to companies having a choice between U.S. GAAP and IFRS, Convergence "giveth and taketh away": the choice that U.S. companies now have because of Convergence will eventually cease to exist because of Convergence.

In the meantime, U.S. companies must choose which path they will travel on the journey to globally converged financial reporting standards. Unfortunately, most U.S. financial managers are not prepared to make an informed choice regarding whether their companies should travel the U.S. GAAP path or the IFRS path. This chapter will provide practical guidance on making that choice and living with the consequences.

Opportunity and Obligation to Choose

With regard to financial reporting standards, the world is moving toward a common destination: the global adoption of a single set of high-quality, country-neutral financial reporting standards. That set of standards is not current U.S. GAAP or current IFRS; it is the future set of standards into which U.S. GAAP and IFRS are converging.

At this point in time, it is possible for different countries and different companies to follow different paths to that common destination. Most countries have chosen to take the IFRS path rather than the U.S. GAAP path. But that does not mean the United States and its companies should or will travel the IFRS path or that all U.S. companies should or will necessarily travel the same path as each other.

In general, the benefits, costs, and risks that a company experiences will differ depending on whether the company chooses the U.S. GAAP path or the IFRS path. The benefits, costs, and risks associated with each set of standards also differ among companies. For example, smaller, domestic, private firms are less likely to experience benefits and more likely to incur disproportionately high costs if they switch from U.S. GAAP to IFRS.

Thus, the optimal choice of a set of financial reporting standards is highly subjective. One choice—say, U.S. GAAP—may be optimal for one company while a different choice—say, IFRS—may be optimal for another company. Furthermore, a particular choice—say, IFRS—may be beneficial for one company but disastrous for another.

Most U.S. companies will find it advantageous to continue using U.S. GAAP indefinitely. A smaller number of U.S. companies will find it advantageous to switch to IFRS—some sooner, some later. And for a certain few U.S. companies, it will be absolutely crucial to switch to IFRS as soon as possible. The key point is that the only way to determine the optimal choice for *your* company is to conduct a thorough investigation of the alternatives, taking your company's unique characteristics and circumstances into consideration. In particular, you should recognize that the "default" option of continuing to use U.S. GAAP may not be the optimal choice for your company. But, in any case, choosing either U.S. GAAP or IFRS will bring new challenges, risks, and consequences that you and your company must be prepared to handle.

How should you go about determining the set of standards that would be best for your company to use in the short run, recognizing that both U.S. GAAP and IFRS will undergo rapid and profound change as they converge with each other in the long run? A methodology for making the optimal choice is explained in the next section.

Methodology for Choosing

The following methodology for determining the optimal set of financial reporting standards that your company should use is derived from a proprietary methodology developed by the author for his firm, Leveraged Logic. The methodology consists of six steps:

Step 1: Define your company's options.
Step 2: Determine who will choose.

Step 3: Establish criteria for choosing.
Step 4: Identify the technical differences among options.
Step 5: Assess the impact of the technical differences among options.
Step 6: Evaluate each option against the established criteria and make your choice.

Although this methodology is designed for situations in which a company has a choice of which financial reporting standards to use, certain steps may be pertinent to situations in which a company is forced to change from one set of standards to another. Specifically, steps 4 and 5 would be helpful in the case of a mandatory conversion, which may be due to changes in securities laws and regulations, changes in a company's ownership, or changes in a company's domicile.

Each of the steps of this methodology is explained in detail in the following subsections. Keep in mind that a company's circumstances may change over time, so executing this methodology should not be viewed as a one-time exercise. It is advisable to repeat the steps at least annually.

Define Your Company's Options

The first step in the methodology for choosing the optimal set of financial reporting standards for your company is to define the options from which your company may choose.

For a U.S. public company, assuming that it will remain under the jurisdiction of the Securities and Exchange Commission (SEC), there are at most two realistic options: current U.S. GAAP and current IFRS. Those options represent the two paths between which U.S. public companies must choose in the short term as public companies worldwide move toward the future set of financial reporting standards into which U.S. GAAP and IFRS are converging.

There are two ways in which switching to current IFRS would be an option for a U.S. public company. The first is the company's satisfying the eligibility criteria established in the IFRS "road map" that has been proposed by the SEC. Eligible U.S. public companies may elect to use current IFRS instead of current U.S. GAAP in preparing the financial reports that those companies must file with the SEC. At the time the SEC voted to issue the proposed road map in August 2008, it was estimated that at least 110 companies would satisfy the eligibility criteria. However, the number of companies that satisfy the eligibility criteria is expected to grow over time due to changing circumstances. Additionally, the SEC may change the eligibility criteria in the future so as to extend eligibility to a greater number of companies.

The second way in which switching to current IFRS would be an option for a U.S. public company is the company's willingness to redomicile in a country that allows or requires current IFRS, becoming what the SEC refers to as a foreign private issuer (FPI). In November 2007, the SEC voted unanimously to accept from FPIs financial statements that are prepared using IFRS as issued by the International Accounting Standards Board (IASB) without reconciliation to U.S. GAAP.

In contrast to U.S. public companies, U.S. private companies face a less certain future with regard to financial reporting standards (see Chapter 6) and have more options from which to choose in the present. Those options include current U.S. GAAP, current IFRS, the current *IFRS for Private Entities*, or any other comprehensive basis of accounting (OCBOA).

Determine Who Will Choose

The second step in the methodology for choosing the optimal set of financial reporting standards for your company is to determine who will actually make the choice. This is a key corporate governance issue. It has been argued that a choice of such significance to a company's owners and other users of financial statements should not be entrusted to the company's management. Some observers have even argued that it would be best if shareholders themselves voted on the choice—after all, who better than the primary users of financial reports to decide which standards serve their needs best?

Ultimately, the "correct" answer to the question of who will choose a company's financial reporting standards is as subjective as the choice of standards itself. But whether the choice is made by the company's management, board of directors, or owners, it is essential that the question be answered up front and that the choice process be highly transparent.

Establish Criteria for Choosing

The third step in this methodology is to establish criteria for choosing among the options that were identified in the first step. This is another key corporate governance issue to be addressed independently of determining who will make the choice.

Ideally, the criteria for choosing a set of financial reporting standards should be established such that the option that best satisfies the criteria will best serve the interests of the company's owners. In order to accomplish that, it may be necessary for the criteria to address the interests of other individuals and entities that participate in the financial reporting supply chain.

At a strategic level, the criteria you establish should relate to preserving and, if possible, enhancing your company's competitive advantage(s). Along those lines, here are some suggested criteria to consider. You should examine each option to understand the extent to which it contributes to:

- Minimizing your company's cost of capital, especially relative to your company's competitors
- Minimizing your company's operating costs and operating complexity
- Minimizing the transitional costs associated with any up-front and on-going changes in standards
- Maximizing the effectiveness of your company's internal control over financial reporting
- Maximizing your company's flexibility with regard to sourcing financial reporting talent

Keep in mind that feasibility constraints must be considered in addition to any evaluative criteria. Such constraints would include, for example, cost constraints and the availability of necessary resources such as qualified financial reporting talent.

Identify the Technical Differences among Options

The fourth step in this methodology is to identify the technical differences among the options that were identified in the first step. In particular, you should seek to understand the standard-level differences among the different sets of financial reporting standards that your company is considering. However, you can ignore differences that are not relevant to your company. Just remember that the differences that are relevant to your company may be more or less relevant to other companies, so you should not rely exclusively on the experience of other companies or on general summaries of differences between particular sets of standards.

The starting point for identifying the relevant technical differences among different sets of standards is your company's current financial accounting and reporting policy manual. Going through that manual policy by policy will provide structure and focus to your efforts to educate yourself regarding the standard-level differences that are most relevant to your company. As you go through each policy, you should refer to the appropriate authoritative standards in each set of standards that your company is considering. Of course, individual standards within any set of financial reporting standards will change over time, and therefore the technical differences among sets of standards will change over time as well, so you should plan to review the differences periodically.

Assess the Impact of the Technical Differences among Options

The fifth step in this methodology is to assess the impact of the technical differences that were identified in the preceding step. Any choice of financial reporting standards that your company makes will have significant financial and operational implications as a result of the unique technical characteristics of each set of standards.

The standard-level differences that you identified in the preceding step are the foundation for this step of the methodology. In this step, you should identify what accounting and reporting policy changes you would be required to make or would desire to make under each different set of standards that your company is considering. Then you should assess the financial and operating impact of any different accounting and reporting policies. The appendix to this chapter contains a checklist of 15 common points of impact that you may find helpful. And involving a broad range of individuals throughout your organization in this step will help to ensure that no impacts are missed.

Evaluate Each Option and Make Your Choice

The sixth and final step in this methodology is to evaluate each option against the established criteria and make a choice based on that evaluation. Once the choice of a set of financial reporting standards is made, the choice must be implemented, as described in the next section.

Implementing Your Choice

As challenging as it will be to choose the optimal set of financial reporting standards for your company to use until the goal of Convergence is attained, it will be equally challenging to implement your choice. The knowledge, skills, and abilities (KSAs) required to do each task, however, differ markedly.

There are two particular areas of KSAs that are needed for the implementation of your choice of a set of financial reporting standards. The first is *risk management* and the second is *project management*. Each is described below.

Risk Management

Risk management starts by asking, "What could go wrong?" From the company's perspective, there are several categories of risks that are associated with implementing a given set of financial reporting standards. Although the risks associated with implementing a choice may vary from option to option, the kinds of risks to be managed during implementation are fairly consistent regardless of what your specific choice is.

Major categories of Convergence risks include:

- Governance risk (e.g., owners and/or directors might not understand the changes that must be made to financial reporting)
- Compliance risk (e.g., your company may fail to comply with unfamiliar financial reporting standards)
- Performance risk (e.g., your company's bottom line may suffer as a result of excessive spending on a transition to another set of standards)
- Audit risk (e.g., your company's auditors might fail to detect material misstatements as a result of unfamiliar standards)
- Usage risk (e.g., users of your company's financial reports may perceive reports prepared under unfamiliar standards to be unreliable)
- Regulatory risk (e.g., government regulators may second-guess preparers' and auditors' decisions under standards that require more extensive exercise of professional judgment)

Note that the risk-management issues of implementing a choice of standards extend far beyond simply assuring compliance with those standards.

Project Management

Project management begins with a very specific goal that must be clear to everyone involved in the project. Working "backward," intermediate milestones should be established on a schedule. And from there, individual subprojects and tasks that must be done to accomplish those milestones should be identified and scheduled as well. Finally, the detailed schedule should be used as the basis of estimating the money and other resources that will be required to ultimately accomplish the project's goal.

Switching to a different set of financial reporting standards is not like a general ledger conversion or enterprise resource planning (ERP) system implementation. It is something that will touch external as well as internal stakeholders in a highly visible, highly significant way. Do not make the mistake of thinking this is simply a technical accounting project. At all times throughout the project, open and frequent communication with the project's stakeholders is essential. In particular, your role as a financial manager must expand to include educating your company's internal and external stakeholders on the rationale for and implications of the technical changes in financial accounting and reporting that are associated with your company's choice of standards.

As much as stakeholders want to know "What's going on?," many will also want to know "How much is this costing us?" Recognize that your estimates of implementation time, complexity, and cost are likely to be low if you are not experienced in managing large-scale, high-impact projects of a technical nature. Therefore, you may wish to engage outside talent to ensure that stakeholder expectations are set appropriately and then met. In any case, recognize that the cost and effort to implement is a function of several subjective factors, including:

- The centralization versus decentralization of your organization
- The robustness of your company's information technology (IT) systems and applications
- The complexity of your company's operations

Conclusion

One clear implication of Convergence is that all companies that use U.S. GAAP today should begin preparing for a future of country-neutral standards. But that does not necessarily mean that all companies face equal opportunities and incentives to switch to current IFRS, nor does it mean that all companies face the same risks and costs.

All U.S. financial managers, however, face the common challenge of helping their companies to make and implement the optimal choice of financial reporting standards, recognizing that any choice is likely to be only temporary as the process of Convergence continues. Greatly complicating the choice is the fact that all sets of standards will change significantly in the future as a result of Convergence. Thus, the subjective benefits, costs, incentives, and risks associated with each option will change over time as well, potentially altering the subjective optimality of each option with the passage of time. Choosing a set of standards is a choice that must be made with an eye to the future as well as the present, and the future always contains an element of uncertainty. That is why the choice of standards should be made within the context of a long-term plan rather than a one-time exercise.

Convergence will be challenging, to a certain extent uncomfortable, and occasionally even painful. You can't avoid it, but you can manage it in a reasonably optimal way.

If you choose not to decide, you still have made a choice.

—Rush, "Freewill"

Appendix: Checklist for Impact Assessment

The following checklist is derived from a proprietary "Convergence Impact Assessment" practice aid developed by the author for his firm, Leveraged Logic. Use this to help you identify what may be impacted by the financial accounting and reporting policies that your company would implement under a given choice of financial reporting standards.

1. Key performance indicators (KPIs) and other performance-evaluation metrics for business units and individuals
2. Compensation plans (including executive compensation plans, profit-sharing plans, sales commissions, and other incentive-based compensation plans)
3. Contingent-compensation arrangements arising from business combinations
4. Loan covenants and other contractual credit agreements
5. Provisions of structured finance instruments
6. Contractual agreements in general (especially government contracts)
7. Dividend policy and statutory limits on dividend-paying ability if reported capital structure changes
8. Disclosures of impact of anticipated change in accounting policies
9. Taxation issues (e.g., deferred tax assets and liabilities, inventory cost flow assumptions)
10. Governance, risk, and compliance (GRC) issues
11. Budgeting and planning processes
12. Other business processes
13. Information systems (especially financial accounting, financial reporting, statutory reporting, other GRC systems)
14. Internal controls over financial reporting and the assessment thereof
15. Statutory reporting and rate-setting issues for companies in regulated industries

CHAPTER 21

Departmental Challenge: Tactics for Managing Talent

This chapter will help you prepare to meet the department-level challenge of managing financial reporting talent in a world of converging financial reporting standards. Preparation is critical because Convergence will require financial managers to change the way they identify, engage, compensate, educate, retain, and supervise their staff personnel.

While a company's switch from current U.S. generally accepted accounting principles (GAAP) to current International Financial Reporting Standards (IFRS) would increase the urgency of addressing the talent-management issues covered in this chapter, keep in mind that managing financial reporting talent in the face of Convergence is not simply about planning for and implementing a one-time transition. In terms of talent management, financial managers will need to plan for continual change and will need to be prepared for a continual transition over many years.

The two main aspects of talent management that financial managers will need to focus on are talent sourcing and technical supervision. In particular, talent sourcing addresses the questions:

- What financial reporting knowledge, skills, and abilities (KSAs) will your department need in order to execute its mission?
- From whom will your department obtain the financial reporting KSAs that it needs?
- How will workers acquire and maintain the necessary financial reporting KSAs?

Each of those questions, along with technical supervision issues, will be examined in the following sections.

Identifying Your Department's Talent Needs

Sourcing financial reporting talent begins with conducting a comprehensive, long-term assessment of your department's talent needs. When identifying your department's present and future needs, it is helpful to differentiate between *ongoing* talent needs and *transitional* talent needs. Ongoing needs relate to the talent required to execute your department's routine business processes. Transitional needs relate to the talent required to execute major change initiatives above and beyond the minor adjustments that must be made to routine business processes from time to time. Of course, Convergence will impact both the ongoing and transitional talent needs of your department.

Within each of those sets of needs, it is helpful to further distinguish between *technical* and *managerial* talent needs. That distinction is an important one with regard to Convergence. Without a doubt, the technical challenges associated with Convergence are big—*but the managerial challenges are even bigger*. Consequently, it is essential that you pay at least as much attention to identifying your department's managerial talent needs as you pay to identifying your department's technical talent needs. And as a manager yourself, striking an appropriate balance between both areas in your own KSAs will help you lead your department and company effectively during the challenging times ahead.

The specific KSAs that a finance department will need to source will vary significantly from company to company. Differences in needs for financial reporting talent among companies will be driven to a large extent by the different choices that companies make regarding which financial reporting standards to use.

Examples of KSAs that your department *might* need to source include the following:

- *Ongoing technical KSAs* may include those related to the measurement of assets and liabilities in accordance with fair-value standards. Relatively few accounting and finance professionals possess such KSAs today. Also, as discussed in previous chapters, any shift away from "following the rules" toward "exercising professional judgment" will require a corresponding shift in financial reporting professionals' KSAs.
- *Ongoing managerial KSAs* would also change as financial reporting managers oversee the work of subordinates who are expected to exercise greater professional judgment than they do today.
- *Transitional technical KSAs* may include those related to the preparation of financial statements in accordance with current IFRS. The need for such KSAs may be only short term and temporary in nature as you develop those KSAs among your permanent staff for the long term.

- *Transitional managerial KSAs* may include those related to project man-agement, change management, and investor relations. *Note that needs for these kinds of nontechnical KSAs are often overlooked by financial managers when conducting talent needs assessments.*

When identifying your department's talent needs—ongoing and transi-tional, technical and managerial—you should recognize that Convergence and other phenomena will cause those needs to change continually over many years regardless of which financial reporting standards your company chooses to use. Thus, managing financial reporting talent effectively will require you to assess your department's talent needs over a relatively long time frame and to reassess those needs periodically.

Specifically, you should identify, quantitatively and qualitatively, the KSAs that your department will require on a year-by-year basis for at least five years. The scope of your talent needs assessment should include all KSAs that you expect your department to need, not just the KSAs af-fected by Convergence. Given that other phenomena such as the Financial Accounting Standards Board's (FASB's) Accounting Standards Codification and eXtensible Business Reporting Language (XBRL) are also dramatically altering the financial reporting talent needs of U.S. companies, it is easy to see that conducting a comprehensive, long-term talent needs assessment for your department will not be a trivial task. Because of that, you may wish to seek help from internal or external human resources professionals.

Assuring the Supply of Talent for Your Department

Once you have assessed the financial reporting KSAs that your department will need to obtain, you must then develop a *talent assurance plan*, that is, a plan to obtain the talent that will provide the needed KSAs. Your talent assurance plan must address the specific manner in which your department intends to identify, engage, compensate, and retain workers who possess the KSAs that your department needs and who therefore represent the talent that you need an assured supply of.

Your talent assurance plan should cover the same multiyear period as your talent needs assessment covers. And just as your department's need for financial reporting KSAs will change during the needs assessment time frame, you can expect the available supply of financial reporting talent to change quantitatively and qualitatively over that time frame as well.

In general, your plan should anticipate talent shortages in the short term followed by talent surpluses in the long term (see Part Three), similar to what happened to the availability of U.S. information technology talent during and following the year 2000 frenzy. In particular, qualified project management talent is likely to be in short supply in the short term, much in the same way that it was during the early years of Sarbanes-Oxley (SOX) implementation.

Also be aware that the availability of talent may vary from company to company. For example, it will be especially difficult for smaller companies to compete effectively for talent during periods of talent shortages.

In preparing your talent assurance plan, you should certainly consider emerging models for sourcing talent via telework arrangements rather than requiring workers to be physically present at a common workplace. Some telework may even be "offshored" on either a contractual or captive basis. In any case, your talent assurance plan should reflect the appropriate use of technology to maximize your sourcing flexibility.

The four activities of identifying, engaging, compensating, and retaining talent represent the core activities of talent sourcing, and a variety of tactics may be employed in performing each activity. The remainder of this section will aid you in creating your talent assurance plan by examining each of the core sourcing activities in detail.

Core Activity 1: Identify

The first of the four core activities of talent sourcing is to identify workers who could potentially provide the financial reporting KSAs that your department needs. Your talent assurance plan should specify how you intend to identify such workers.

In general, you should plan to look for talent within your department, then within your company, then outside your company, in that order. Remember that as a result of Convergence, the talent supply pipeline(s) that your department has traditionally relied on may prove decreasingly capable of furnishing your department with the quantity and quality of talent that you seek. Therefore, you should be ready to expand the geographic scope of your talent sourcing practices to include additional labor markets and their associated pipelines as needed. In general, you should plan to participate in the most competitive labor markets in which you are able to participate.

Knowing where to look is only one part of the talent assurance plan, however. When it comes to identifying talent, it will also be necessary for you to discriminate among potential workers in the talent pool on the basis of the KSAs that they possess. However, be aware that Convergence may invalidate some traditional indicators of talent quality:

Because Convergence is obsolescing KSAs at a rapid rate, the amount of a worker's past experience may have little to do with how likely the worker is to possess the newer KSAs that your department needs. Younger professionals who have less overall experience may actually be better hires if their experience is more relevant than that of older professionals who have more overall experience.

The credentials that your department has traditionally relied on in identifying suitable candidates may be decreasingly applicable to your department's KSA needs. As discussed in Chapter 18, you should be aware of newer credentials that attest to KSAs that may be more relevant to your department's needs than the KSAs that traditional credentials attest to.

Another consideration is that as Convergence progresses, talent hired out of large public accounting firms will be much more likely than talent hired out of smaller public accounting firms to possess the financial reporting KSAs that hiring companies need. This will be the inevitable result of the formal Convergence-related training and development efforts that the large firms have recently undertaken in earnest and that smaller firms lack the resources to undertake, at least in the short term.

Finally, one of the biggest challenges in identifying talent over the next several years will arise from the anticipated shift to less-rules-based financial reporting standards as a result of Convergence. It will certainly be more difficult for companies to assess the quality of professional judgment among prospective workers, especially since it is not likely to be high for any U.S. worker in the pool of candidates.

Core Activity 2: Engage

The second of the four core activities of talent sourcing is to engage workers whom you have identified as potential providers of the financial reporting KSAs that your department needs. Your talent assurance plan should specify how you intend to engage such workers.

There are four generic tactics for engaging the talent that you need. Each can be referred to by a word that is more commonly used to refer to obtaining the use of physical assets. But the same concepts underlie engaging human talent, and the hierarchy of desirability among the tactics is the same as well. And so, when looking to engage talent, think "Borrow-Rent-Buy-Build," in that order.

- "Borrowing" talent refers to obtaining a worker on a temporary basis from elsewhere within your company. An example would be to have an employee from a foreign affiliate temporarily assigned to your department. This is often the quickest, least risky, and least costly tactic for engaging workers, which is why it is the most desirable of the tactics. Unfortunately, it is rarely a feasible option, especially in smaller companies.
- "Renting" talent refers to obtaining a worker on a temporary basis from outside your company in a contractual relationship of limited scope. An example would be engaging a contact worker to assist in a general ledger conversion. "Renting" can be a quick, low-risk method of engagement, but it clearly imposes incremental costs on the client company and is inappropriate for long-term talent needs.

- "Buying" talent refers to obtaining a worker on a long-term basis through an employer-employee relationship. This method of engagement tends to require more recruitment time, effort, and cost up front, and generally commits the employer to substantial costs over the long term.
- "Building" talent refers to providing current and/or prospective employees with educational opportunities that are intended to convey certain KSAs to those employees. For example, you might arrange for your staff to participate in webcasts covering new KSAs that they will soon be expected to possess. Also, you might provide technical and financial support to college accounting departments (especially at institutions from which your company recruits) in order to ensure that entry-level workers have the KSAs that your company needs. You may even choose to invest in increasing foreign workers' English proficiency and familiarity with U.S. business practices.

Of all the engagement tactics, "building" tends to be the least desirable among employers because it takes the most time and is the most risky. One risk is that educational initiatives may fail to achieve their goals. Another risk is that once workers have acquired valuable KSAs through company-sponsored education, those newly upgraded workers may choose to seek employment with another company offering higher compensation.

So when should a company plan to use the "build" tactic? When the company believes that is will be impossible or more costly to implement the other tactics. During the anticipated short-term period of financial reporting talent shortages, "building" the necessary talent for your department may be the only feasible option, so you should at least consider incorporating it into your talent assurance plan.

Core Activity 3: Compensate

The third of the four core activities of talent sourcing is setting the compensation of the financial reporting workers that you wish to engage or that you have engaged. Your talent assurance plan should specify compensation levels that have a reasonable expectation of acceptance by workers and that represent a cost that is proportionate to the benefits to the company from engaging those workers.

You should be aware that global shortages of financial reporting talent in the short term may cause compensation levels among financial reporting workers to rise significantly. But you should also be aware that the long-term trend in compensation is exactly the opposite—your company will eventually be able to pay much less than it pays now for financial reporting talent. In every case, a thorough knowledge of compensation levels within multiple labor markets will prove very helpful in minimizing compensation costs for a given set of financial reporting KSAs.

Core Activity 4: Retain

Finally, the fourth core activity of talent sourcing is retaining workers whom you want to retain. Those are the workers who have demonstrated that they possess the KSAs that your department needs and are willing to provide at a cost that makes sense for your company. But as workers acquire new financial reporting KSAs in response to Convergence, there is a real risk that workers who possess KSAs that are in high demand will be tempted to seek "greener pastures" as they realize and exploit their bargaining power in the short term.

Thus, retaining qualified staff is likely to be a particular challenge in the short term. The more in touch you are with what your workers want out of their relationship with your company, the more likely you are to develop effective ways to retain those workers.

Training and Development

To the extent that you choose the "build" tactic for engaging your department's financial reporting talent, you should prepare a plan for training and development.[1] That plan will focus on the education of specific individuals whom you expect your department to employ on a long-term basis.

Preparing a training and development plan starts with a "gap analysis," that is, identifying differences between the KSAs that your employees have and the KSAs that your department needs them to have. The plan then details how the gaps will be closed through specific educational experiences, which may be a blend of on-the-job learning and more structured methods. This section will provide you with numerous concepts and ideas that will help you develop a training and development plan for your department.

General Planning Considerations

There are four general considerations for you to think about as you prepare your training and development plan:

1. The effectiveness of training and development is heavily dependent on timing. For maximum effectiveness, training and development should be delivered on a "just in time" (JIT) basis, that is, immediately before a worker will be required to put his or her newly acquired KSAs into practice. Most companies, however, find it nearly impossible to deliver

training and development on a JIT basis. Adding to the difficulty is the fact that Convergence will in most cases require such a large amount of training and development that the learning process must necessarily begin well before it ends, which increases the risk that KSAs acquired early in the learning process will be lost by the end of the learning process as a result of not being put to immediate use. Consequently, for any long-duration educational activities in your training and development plan, you should add extra "practice" activities throughout the learning process specifically to assure the retention of KSAs that are acquired long before they will actually be applied on the job.

2. The composition of your department's staff will change over time, so your overall training and development plan should incorporate contingent elements for responding to the potential loss of key employees. It should also reflect the potential need to supplement the KSAs of new employees whom you anticipate hiring but who may not have all of the KSAs that you ultimately want them to have.

3. You should anticipate resistance to Convergence-related training and development from sources of funding within your company. Your boss may argue that "none of this stuff is value adding" and that employees will "jump ship after we train them." The key to overcoming such resistance is being able to demonstrate that other engagement tactics would be more costly, not timely enough, or simply not feasible to implement.

4. As a result of creating your training and development plan, you may find that Convergence-related education will occupy a substantial portion of your employees' jobs—so much so that you will need to add temporary talent during the educational process in order for the real work of your department to keep getting done.

Content Considerations

When it comes to planning the content of Convergence-related training and development, here are some key points to keep in mind:

- Do not assume that everyone on your staff has a need to know the technical differences between current U.S. GAAP and current IFRS. Unless your company has immediate plans to switch from current U.S. GAAP to current IFRS in the short term, such education will be wasted on rank-and-file accountants because both sets of standards will change significantly as they converge with each other.
- If your employees do need to learn current IFRS in order to perform their jobs, then they are likely to need to become fluent in IFRS. Fluency

in IFRS is most effectively attained by immersive education in "pure" IFRS, not by studying the differences between IFRS and U.S. GAAP.

- The training and development needs of managers, such as yourself, will differ from the training and development needs of employees who have task-level responsibility for financial reporting. In particular, financial executives *will* need to be educated in the technical differences between current U.S. GAAP and current IFRS in order to be able to assess whether their companies should switch to current IFRS.
- Regardless of whether your company uses U.S. GAAP or IFRS in the short term, Convergence will require all department personnel to continually update their KSAs as each set of standards undergoes profound change.

Educational Methods

In addition to specifying educational content, your training and development plan should specify the educational methods that will be used to convey the content to employees. Training and development in financial reporting KSAs can encompass a variety of educational methods including structured classroom instruction, computer-based self-study, informal on-the-job learning experiences, and others.

With regard to Convergence, certain training and development methods are likely to be more effective and less costly than others. For example, self-study programs can be cost-effective in general, but when they are based on a body of KSAs that will change as frequently as Convergence will force financial reporting KSAs to change, those programs invariably suffer from a severe lack of timeliness. And while face-to-face seminars tend to be very effective from an educational perspective, they are very expensive in terms of:

- Direct out-of-pocket costs (for the seminars themselves)
- Indirect out-of-pocket costs (for transportation, lodging, etc.)
- Opportunity costs (travel and seminar time away from work)

But once again, technology is a key enabler of business success. For example, live webcasts retain the benefits of instructor-led education while minimizing the costs of obtaining those benefits. Thus, your training and development plan should reflect the appropriate use of technology to maximize educational effectiveness while minimizing cost.

On-the-Job versus Formal Continuing Education

As noted in Chapter 18, there are two primary categories of education for working professionals: on-the-job education and formal continuing education. On-the-job education often involves employees within the company who already possess certain KSAs teaching other employees who lack those KSAs. But as Convergence obsolesces the financial reporting KSAs of everyone in a department and simultaneously imposes similar learning needs on everyone, there is less opportunity for employees to help each other. Thus, Convergence is likely to increase the need for formal continuing education with regard to financial reporting KSAs. But that does not mean on-the-job education has no place in your training and development plan. You should still look for opportunities to arrange on-the-job learning experiences where possible and periodically debrief employees to gauge the effectiveness of those experiences.

Additionally, if your company is large enough, you may wish to consider establishing a Convergence "center of excellence" or "community of practice" to leverage the benefits of on-the-job learning across the entire company. If certain employees possess a significantly larger set of relevant KSAs that other employees lack, you may want to consider making it a formal part of the more capable employees' jobs to lead the learning of less capable employees, either through on-the-job educational experiences or more structured ones.

If your company is smaller, you will probably have to rely more on outside talent, outside coaching, and "study groups" composed of employees spanning multiple companies. And OFOs (only financial officers) may have no choice but to rely more on formal continuing education than their counterparts in larger companies will.

Technical Supervision

Financial managers will face additional Convergence-related talent-management challenges beyond those associated with talent sourcing. Specifically, Convergence will change the nature of day-to-day supervision of workers who perform the technical aspects of financial reporting work. You can expect this to be true with regard to both the ongoing and transitional talent that you will supervise.

One challenge arises from the fact that in the short term you will probably not possess significantly greater technical KSAs in financial reporting than the workers that you supervise will possess, as noted in "On-the-Job versus Formal Continuing Education" above. This is a direct result of the rapid obsolescence of the financial reporting KSAs possessed by U.S. workers—including financial managers. As greater tenure ceases to imply more relevant expertise, the hierarchy of technical expertise within your department will flatten, and the "pecking order" will become more ambiguous.

Other emerging supervisory challenges include:

- As the geographic scope of your permanent and temporary staff expands, you may find yourself facing cross-cultural issues in supervising foreign workers.
- Supervising a geographically distributed workforce is definitely more challenging than supervising workers face to face.
- The anticipated shift toward the increased exercise of professional judgment in financial reporting work will significantly alter the nature of technical supervision.

Conclusion

Convergence will change labor markets for financial reporting talent and will change the talent pipelines that supply those markets. As a result, your department will face new choices and new challenges in sourcing its financial reporting talent. You are also likely to experience a change in the nature of your supervisory role. All this comes when your company's competitors are struggling with the same challenges and may enjoy considerable competitive advantages if they master those challenges sooner and/or better than you and your company do.

To summarize what you should do to prepare for managing financial reporting talent, you should first conduct a talent needs assessment. Next, you should develop a talent assurance plan. Then you should develop a training and development plan. Finally, you should implement your talent assurance and training and development plans, with the understanding that the longer you wait to do so, the bigger the head start you give to your company's competitors.

Note

1. While the terms *training* and *development* may seem redundant when used in conjunction with each other, as they so often are, the terms in fact differ from each other in that training focuses on the KSAs that workers must possess in order to perform their current jobs, whereas development focuses on the KSAs that workers must possess in order to be capable of performing different jobs, either now or in the future. The common phrase *training* and *development* simply reflects that fact that it often makes sense to plan and implement both activities together within a department or company.

CHAPTER 22

Personal Challenge: Career Choices for a Hypercompetitive Labor Market

This chapter, like Chapter 21, expands on concepts that were introduced in Part Three, which described the short- and long-term impacts of Convergence on U.S. labor markets for financial reporting talent. While those impacts certainly have significant managerial implications (as discussed in Chapter 21), they also have significant personal career implications for U.S. financial managers.

In particular, as Convergence transforms labor markets throughout the world, it threatens to undermine the employability and earning power of individual accounting and finance professionals, especially in the United States. The purpose of this chapter is to help you preserve your employability while bolstering your ability to compete effectively for new career opportunities in an increasingly competitive, globalized labor market. You will learn what career choices you must be prepared to make—and why—in order to address the "personal challenge" of Convergence.

Hypercompetition in a Global Labor Market

For financial managers working in the United States, career success can be very rewarding. It often translates into personal prosperity, security, and fulfillment. But career success is becoming more difficult for U.S. financial managers to attain as a result of Convergence.

Recall from Part Three that Convergence is transforming the world's labor markets for financial reporting talent. In the short run, that transformation will result in new, lucrative career opportunities for accounting and finance professionals who choose to prepare themselves now for the impact of Convergence. In the long run, however, professionals in the United States and throughout the world will find themselves with more rivals for fewer jobs at lower wages in the emerging global labor market for financial reporting talent.

For all the reasons described in Part Three, it will eventually become very difficult for individual financial professionals to distinguish themselves in the eyes of their present and prospective employers. It will also be very difficult for U.S. professionals to command the premium wages—relative to the rest of the world—that they have been accustomed to. Consequently, U.S. financial managers should start preparing themselves now if they wish to have any chance of succeeding in the emerging hypercompetitive, global labor market for financial reporting talent.

Alternatively, some of today's financial managers may decide that it is simply not worth the time and effort to prepare for the impact that Convergence will have on their careers. Many are inclined to say, "I'd rather retire than deal with new challenges," which include not only the impact of Convergence but also the effects of other phenomena such as the Financial Accounting Standards Board's (FASB's) Accounting Standards Codification and eXtensible Business Reporting Language (XBRL) as well. An "exit strategy" is certainly a valid response to what is happening, but if you choose that strategy, you will soon be out of the game permanently. Teaching accounting classes, mentoring younger professionals, and other professionally related activities that you may have contemplated in retirement or semiretirement simply will not be options for you as you will lack the technical knowledge, skills, and abilities (KSAs) relevant to the next generation.

Managing Your Career

If you choose to stay in the game, there are three "must do's" for dealing effectively with the rapid and profound changes that Convergence is bringing to your career:

1. *Take stock.* Assess your situation. Recognize that you will soon need to upgrade your KSAs in order to compete with other individual professionals on a global scale, and recognize that the competition will only get more intense over time.
2. *Take responsibility.* Do not rely on anyone else to manage your career or to make decisions regarding your professional development. As a competitor in a global, high-stakes game, you should commit yourself

to pursuing and winning the career opportunities that will benefit you the most.

3. *Take action*. The best time to act is now. Chances are that you are already at a disadvantage in the hiring factors that will become increasingly important to employers over time. If you wait until you absolutely, positively have to be on board the "Convergence" train, you may find that it has already left the station without you.

In specific terms, you should strive to:

1. Be relevant.
2. Be visible.
3. Be distinct.
4. Be flexible.

Each of these four objectives will now be discussed in detail.

Be Relevant

Due to the trends described in Chapter 15, more and more financial management jobs require professionals to possess KSAs that extend beyond those based solely on U.S. generally accepted accounting principles (GAAP). Unfortunately, financial professionals in the United States rarely possess such KSAs since they are not commonly taught in college accounting curricula and are not tested on professional certification examinations that are common in the United States. The fact that non-U.S. professionals increasingly possess the KSAs demanded by U.S. employers puts further pressure on U.S. professionals to remain relevant to employers in terms of acquiring additional KSAs.

Recognize, however, that relevant KSAs are of little value unless you can prove that you possess them. Therefore, now is the time to reexamine your professional credentials. Do they help convey to employers that you possess KSAs that are relevant in a world of global markets and global financial reporting standards? Credentials that are country specific (or worse, state specific) and that are limited to country-specific KSAs are destined to become anachronisms in our increasingly global business environment. In contrast, credentials that are based on country-neutral financial reporting standards and that are granted by global credentialing bodies send a clear signal of relevance with regard to your KSAs.[1]

Along with your professional credentials, you should plan to actively pursue career opportunities that will enable you to gain experience in areas of growing demand. Drifting through your career and hoping for the best will not work any longer.

Be Visible

Few financial managers—and few professionals who hope to become financial managers—realize that the number one threat to their careers is a *lack of visibility*. Most managers and would-be managers are so afraid of having their failures seen by others that they deliberately choose to keep a low profile within their organizations and the larger professional community. However, choosing invisibility is tantamount to career suicide in a hypercompetitive labor market.

Your goal should be precisely the opposite: to be seen and known by as many people as possible who can help you in your career. Of course, this requires effort, but the tasks before you are straightforward. They include cultivating a network both inside and outside of your organization. Using Internet-based social networking services like LinkedIn is a good start, but face-to-face events sponsored by professional associations provide an even better environment in which to expand your network. And if a professional association is global in scope and actively working to remain relevant in a global business environment,[2] all the better for you. Keep in mind, though, that while networking with peers is desirable, networking with people who have the ability to advance your career is essential.

Other avenues to improving your visibility include:

- Giving presentations.
- Writing articles and/or maintaining an online blog.
- Serving on a committee or project team within a professional association.
- Being a media resource.

In general, you should seek to maximize the number of people who know who you are and what kinds of problems you have solved for your clients and/or employers. Work on your ability to tell truthful, compelling stories about how you solved those problems and never miss an opportunity to tell those stories to people who make or influence hiring decisions, even if you are not currently looking for a job.

Be Distinct

If you cannot cite at least one compelling reason why an employer should choose you over other professionals who are also relevant and visible to that employer, then you have not achieved a necessary measure of *distinction*. Unfortunately, from a career perspective, being distinct will be an increasingly challenging goal for financial professionals. There are relatively few ways to achieve distinction in a commodity market other than by charging the lowest price—and U.S. wage levels are not anywhere near being the lowest in the increasingly commoditized global labor market for financial reporting talent.

One of the few ways to be distinct is to be "first," that is, to be relevant and visible sooner that everyone else with whom you are competing. Having a head start is distinguishing in itself, but it also provides you with an opportunity to maintain your initial advantage of having a greater amount of relevant experience than the majority of your competitors, which in turn will help you stand out from those competitors. The most difficult need for employers to meet is the need for experienced workers—the more experience that an employer seeks, the more difficult it is for the employer to fill the position. Of course, in their quest for experienced workers, employers are expanding the scope of their searches to encompass the global pool of financial reporting talent, and it is all too easy to blend in with the masses. Keep in mind that the large amount of general professional experience that you may currently possess no longer implies relevance. It is essential that your experience be relevant to the continually changing needs of employers, which is why you can ill afford to ignore those needs.

A second way to be distinct is to be an expert. Being an expert implies specializing. It will be far better for you to be recognized as excellent at one thing than to be recognized as merely above average at many things. But understand that being an expert does not mean you have to know everything about a particular subject. What it means is that you must know more than everyone else and that you must be able to find out the things that you do not currently know.

In summary, being distinct is largely about being the first and/or being the best. *Not* being distinct will soon cease to be an option for anyone who wishes to attain the rewards of career success in an increasingly challenging environment.

Be Flexible

Whether you are a contract worker or a "W-2" employee, do not expect any job to last forever. As you have seen, employers' needs for financial reporting talent will change quantitatively and qualitatively at an accelerating pace in the coming years. And so, your fourth objective should be to remain flexible. Make a point of being aware of—and being ready to pursue—beneficial career opportunities as they arise. In a rapidly changing, hypercompetitive market, flexibility is a major competitive advantage.

Conclusion

As you contemplate your future career prospects in a world of converging financial reporting standards, you may feel overwhelmed by the changes around you and by the personal changes that will be required to continue earning a living as a financial professional. Fortunately, your future career success is not beyond reach; it will, however, require you to make choices and take action in ways that are probably new to you. Along with millions of other financial professionals throughout the world in essentially the same boat, what you do or do not do now in response to the personal challenge of Convergence will determine your career opportunities and rewards for years to come.

Notes

1. The most prominent example of a credential based on country-neutral financial reporting standards and granted by a global credentialing body is the Diploma in International Financial Reporting (DipIFR), granted by the Association of Chartered Certified Accountants (ACCA).
2. Examples of such organizations include Financial Executives International (FEI), the Institute of Management Accountants (IMA), and the ACCA.

Part IV Epilogue

This final part has provided practical guidance on overcoming the three main challenges that Convergence will impose on corporate financial managers. Consider the chapters that you have just read to be the foundation for your own unique, evolving process of preparing for those challenges and other challenges ahead. You will never regret anything you do from this point forward to prepare yourself, your department, and your company for a future in which everything you know about corporate financial reporting today will become obsolete.

To keep up with the latest Convergence developments and their implications for corporate financial managers, visit **TheConvergenceGuidebook.com**.

Index